Afghanistan

Other books in the Current Controversies series:

Afghanistan

Jann Einfeld, *Book Editor*

Bruce Glassman, *Vice President*
Bonnie Szumski, *Publisher*
Helen Cothran, *Managing Editor*

CURRENT CONTROVERSIES

GREENHAVEN PRESS

An imprint of Thomson Gale, a part of The Thomson Corporation

Detroit • New York • San Francisco • San Diego • New Haven, Conn.
Waterville, Maine • London • Munich

4-14-05

THOMSON

GALE

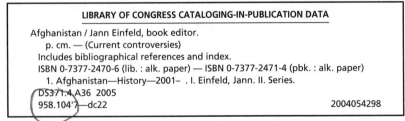

LIBRARY OF CONGRESS CATALOGING-IN-PUBLICATION DATA

Afghanistan / Jann Einfeld, book editor.
    p. cm. — (Current controversies)
    Includes bibliographical references and index.
    ISBN 0-7377-2470-6 (lib. : alk. paper) — ISBN 0-7377-2471-4 (pbk. : alk. paper)
    1. Afghanistan—History—2001– . I. Einfeld, Jann. II. Series.
    DS371.4.A36 2005
    958.104'7—dc22   2004054298

Printed in the United States of America

Contents

No: The Situation in Afghanistan Is Deteriorating

Chapter 2: Has the Human Rights Situation in Afghanistan Improved Since the Fall of the Taliban?

Yes: The Human Rights Situation Has Improved

five hundred wells, and funded income-generating activities to help the
returnees reintegrate into Afghan life.

No: The Human Rights Situation Has Not Improved

Chapter 3: Should the United States and the International Community Continue to Play an Active Role in Afghanistan?

Yes: The United States and the International Community Should Continue to Support Afghanistan's Reconstruction

economic freedom is a necessity. Experience shows that advanced political institutions do not equate with sound economic performance, but free markets and private property rights inevitably lead to increased affluence.

Foreword

By definition, controversies are "discussions of questions in which opposing opinions clash" (Webster's Twentieth Century Dictionary Unabridged). Few would deny that controversies are a pervasive part of the human condition and exist on virtually every level of human enterprise. Controversies transpire between individuals and among groups, within nations and between nations. Controversies supply the grist necessary for progress by providing challenges and challengers to the status quo. They also create atmospheres where strife and warfare can flourish. A world without controversies would be a peaceful world; but it also would be, by and large, static and prosaic.

The Series' Purpose

The purpose of the Current Controversies series is to explore many of the social, political, and economic controversies dominating the national and international scenes today. Titles selected for inclusion in the series are highly focused and specific. For example, from the larger category of criminal justice, Current Controversies deals with specific topics such as police brutality, gun control, white collar crime, and others. The debates in Current Controversies also are presented in a useful, timeless fashion. Articles and book excerpts included in each title are selected if they contribute valuable, long-range ideas to the overall debate. And wherever possible, current information is enhanced with historical documents and other relevant materials. Thus, while individual titles are current in focus, every effort is made to ensure that they will not become quickly outdated. Books in the Current Controversies series will remain important resources for librarians, teachers, and students for many years.

In addition to keeping the titles focused and specific, great care is taken in the editorial format of each book in the series. Book introductions and chapter prefaces are offered to provide background material for readers. Chapters are organized around several key questions that are answered with diverse opinions representing all points on the political spectrum. Materials in each chapter include opinions in which authors clearly disagree as well as alternative opinions in which authors may agree on a broader issue but disagree on the possible solutions. In this way, the content of each volume in Current Controversies mirrors the mosaic of opinions encountered in society. Readers will quickly realize that there are many viable answers to these complex issues. By questioning each author's conclusions, students and casual readers can begin to develop the critical thinking skills so important to evaluating opinionated material.

Current Controversies is also ideal for controlled research. Each anthology in the series is composed of primary sources taken from a wide gamut of informational categories including periodicals, newspapers, books, United States and foreign government documents, and the publications of private and public organizations. Readers will find factual support for reports, debates, and research papers covering all areas of important issues. In addition, an annotated table of contents, an index, a book and periodical bibliography, and a list of organizations to contact are included in each book to expedite further research.

Perhaps more than ever before in history, people are confronted with diverse and contradictory information. During the Persian Gulf War, for example, the public was not only treated to minute-to-minute coverage of the war, it was also inundated with critiques of the coverage and countless analyses of the factors motivating U.S. involvement. Being able to sort through the plethora of opinions accompanying today's major issues, and to draw one's own conclusions, can be a complicated and frustrating struggle. It is the editors' hope that Current Controversies will help readers with this struggle.

Greenhaven Press anthologies primarily consist of previously published material taken from a variety of sources, including periodicals, books, scholarly journals, newspapers, government documents, and position papers from private and public organizations. These original sources are often edited for length and to ensure their accessibility for a young adult audience. The anthology editors also change the original titles of these works in order to clearly present the main thesis of each viewpoint and to explicitly indicate the opinion presented in the viewpoint. These alterations are made in consideration of both the reading and comprehension levels of a young adult audience. Every effort is made to ensure that Greenhaven Press accurately reflects the original intent of the authors included in this anthology.

"The events of September 11, 2001, led to the growing recognition that . . . the safety of world citzenry is in jeopardy as long as the suffering of people in countries such as Afghanistan creates conditions conducive to terrorists."

Introduction

The terrorist attacks of September 11, 2001, signaled the beginning of a new era of hope for the people of Afghanistan. As the home base of the al Qaeda terrorists responsible for the attacks, Afghanistan captured world attention. The United States reversed years of disinterest in central Asian affairs and led a major international effort to oust the Taliban regime, which was harboring al Qaeda, and liberate the Afghan people from fear, oppression, and poverty. President George W. Bush promised that America would reconstruct Afghanistan so it would never again harbor terrorists who would threaten the safety of the Afghan and American people. "We'll . . . rout out the al-Qaeda killers," said Bush, "not only to make sure that Afghanistan is more safe, but also to make sure America is safe as well."

In his comment Bush overtly acknowledged the link between the safety and security of the people in Afghanistan and the safety and security of Americans at home. As long as the Afghan people lived in conditions conducive to the growth of terrorism—namely poverty and instability—Americans remained vulnerable to terrorist assaults. Afghanistan's ambassador to the United States, Said Tayeb Jawad, supported Bush's conclusion: "Our two nations have been . . . victimized by terrorism. . . . On the tragic day of September 11, 2001, the destinies of our countries were joined."

Concern for the mutual security of the American and Afghan people prompted the U.S. government to send air and ground troops to Afghanistan in October 2001. By year's end U.S. and coalition forces had destroyed al Qaeda terrorist cells in the northern mountains and defeated the Taliban. As 2002 dawned, thousands of international aid workers swarmed into Afghanistan eager to help the reconstruction efforts of the new interim Afghan government.

Afghan government and foreign aid officials faced tremendous challenges: Afghanistan's physical infrastructure and human resources had been decimated during the Soviet occupation of the 1970s and 1980s and nearly a decade of civil war under Taliban rule. The country's roads, railways, and cities were in ruins. More than 1.5 million Afghan lives had been lost during those decades, and about one-third of the population became refugees, scattered throughout the region and the world. There were no national institutions and no educated people to staff them, the educated elite having long ago fled to safer shores. Half a million Afghan amputees, casualties of Soviet land mines, remained a visible symbol of the war years.

Reconstruction workers were further challenged by the country's limited natural resources and undeveloped human potential. Indeed, Afghanistan had few natural endowments on which to base a modern economy. The most profitable export—opium, which had supplied most of Europe's heroin addicts for decades—was the target of eradication efforts by the international community. The development of alternative export commodities had been neglected during the war years, as had been Afghanistan's human resources: Less than 10 percent of Afghans were literate, the result of generations of children who had no opportunity to attend school. One in five children died of disease or malnourishment before turning five, and the survivors could expect to live to about forty-eight, which ranks among the lowest life expectancies in the world.

To add to these challenges, in 2001 Afghanistan had experienced its most severe drought in a decade. Government and foreign aid personnel were forced to divert scarce financial resources to help millions of Afghans survive the winter. Their task was complicated by the influx of 2.5 million weary refugees returning home from camps in neighboring countries. Despite these challenges and setbacks, in 2002 the Afghan government and foreign aid donors launched an ambitious program to rebuild the economy, develop national institutions, provide education and health services, eradicate the narcotics trade, and combat human rights abuses.

By early 2003 the effectiveness of these government and aid donor programs became the subject of vigorous debate. Some commentators said that the government and foreign donors had made great progress, pointing to the 30 percent economic growth rate, the new highways and buildings, the 4 million boys and girls going to school, and the 2004 constitution guaranteeing human rights. They argued that the return of 2.5 million refugees from seventeen countries was testament to the new hope that the Afghan people had for their future. Testifying before the U.S. House Committee on International Relations in 2003, State Department official Christina Rocca said,

> Today . . . Afghans enjoy restored liberties that were unheard of in recent memory. An internationally recognized government is in power; schools have reopened, a new banking law is in place, businesses are blossoming around the country; and, most importantly, there is hope for a better future.

Other commentators, however, said that two years after the U.S. invasion the Afghan people had lost hope, the government was unpopular and ineffectual, the U.S.-backed warlords still repressed the people, particularly women, and the foreign aid programs failed to help the poorest Afghans.

By the end of 2003, however, the debate over the country's progress was overshadowed by concern for the deteriorating security situation. Even the most optimistic observers grew alarmed at the increase in lawlessness, the reports of human rights abuses, the booming opium trade, and the resurgence of terrorist violence. Taliban and al Qaeda forces had surreptitiously regrouped in the back country of Pakistan. Returning to Afghanistan, they burned down girls' schools, assassinated government ministers, murdered foreign and local aid workers, and threatened voters registering for the 2004 national election. In February 2004 Taliban leader Mullah Abdullah sent an e-mail to the Islamic press stating,

> If the people of Afghanistan participate in the [2004 national] election, they will come under Taliban attack. . . . We will [also] kill all those Muslims who are working with America and its fifty-two other non-Muslim countries. For every part of the road they asphalt, they make 300 Muslims non-Muslim. We will build our country on Islam, not with road building.

By March 2004, when Afghan government officials met with international aid representatives in Berlin, Germany, they reported that the security situation was spiraling out of control. Without stronger security, they said, the reconstruction program would be crippled and the national election sabotaged by Taliban violence. Afghan president Hamid Karzai urged international donors to increase their involvement in Afghanistan to combat the terrorist revival. "We must defeat the forces and ideas of violence," said the president, "or risk [Afghanistan's] return to drugs, corruption, and terror."

As 2004 progressed, participants and observers debated how Afghanistan should respond to the resurgence of terrorist violence. Afghan government officials said that the United States and other donors must send in more troops to restore the peace and ensure a fair democratic election. They urged donors to accelerate the reconstruction effort to win the hearts and minds of the local people away from the propaganda of the fundamentalists. The fundamentalists, on the other hand, said that the foreign presence was provoking the violence, and that America and the international community should let the Afghans solve their own problems. Islam, they insisted, rather than Western democracy and capitalism, would be the salvation of the Afghan people.

Controversy was not confined to the Afghan community. Western observers heatedly debated the role that the United States should play in Afghanistan. Some commentators said the United States should withdraw since America had not succeeded in restoring the peace or in helping the Afghan people. They said that the United States was provoking more violence by becoming entangled in conflicts in remote corners of the world.

Other Western analysts, however, said that America must stay involved in Afghanistan and argued that Afghanistan would fail without U.S. aid. Some analysts claimed that the September 11, 2001, tragedy was due in large part to U.S. support for Islamic militants during the Soviet occupation. These commentators also blamed America's failure to honor its promises to help reconstruct Afghanistan when the Soviets withdrew. They said that America must take responsibility for past wrongs to maintain its credibility as an ally. "If we fail in Afghanistan, if we let the people of Afghanistan down," said Senator Chuck Hagel from Nebraska, "it will send the message across the globe that you cannot count on our commitment, and you risk, at your peril, associating with the United States."

By late 2004 Afghanistan had reached a crossroads: The country could move forward toward democracy and progress or return to the anarchy and terrorist violence of the past. Failure to restore the peace in Afghanistan would destabilize the region and invite the return of terrorists intent on striking Western targets. Karzai (who was elected Afghanistan's president in the October 2004 national election) warned, "As long as terrorism survives in this part of the world, neither Afghanistan, nor our neighbors, nor indeed the rest of the world can be safe."

The events of September 11, 2001, led to the growing recognition that the countries and the peoples of the world are interdependent, and that the safety of world citizenry is in jeopardy as long as the suffering of people in countries such as Afghanistan creates conditions conducive to terrorists. Barnett Rubin, one of America's foremost central Asian scholars, echoes the views of many observers when he concludes that the victory in the war on terror must begin in Afghanistan. In *The Fragmentation of Afghanistan*, he contends:

> September 11 [2001] showed that . . . the interdependence of all human beings has become a fact that we ignore at our peril. . . . The devastation of Afghanistan enabled outlaws to establish a base for a global network that preys on the suffering of millions. . . . The ultimate test of our globalized [interdependent] world will not be on the streets outside a meeting of the World Trade Organization but in the mountains of Afghanistan.

Chapter 1

Has Afghanistan Made Progress Since the U.S.-Led War Against the Taliban?

Overview: Achievements and Challenges in Postwar Afghanistan

by Ray Salvatore Jennings

About the author: *Ray Salvatore Jennings is the chief of Iraq affairs at the U.S. Institute of Peace in Washington, D.C. Specializing in postconflict reconstruction in war-torn societies, he has worked for the World Bank in Afghanistan and for the U.S. Agency for International Development in Bosnia-Herzegovina, Serbia, Peru, Sierra Leone, and Macedonia.*

Afghanistan's extended civil war began in 1978 and persisted for more than two decades. During that period, war and natural disasters created the single largest refugee caseload in the world for twenty straight years. An estimated 1.5 million people died, and an additional 500,000 were disabled or injured and more than 1 million Afghans were internally displaced. Particularly intense fighting beginning with the collapse of President Muhammad Najibullah's government in 1992 led to severe deterioration of what remained of the political, social, and economic infrastructure of the country. In September 2001, fighting between the two latest combatants in the long war was still under way, with strong advances by the Taliban in the north causing rival Northern Alliance forces to retreat.

On October 7, however, U.S. airstrikes began on Taliban targets in Afghanistan, launched in response to al Qaeda attacks in Washington, D.C., and New York.[1] By mid-December, the Taliban were in disarray and the anti-Taliban Northern Alliance had occupied Kabul. Al Qaeda and most of the Taliban's top leadership had fled the country. In the aftermath, postwar security and the for-

---

1. Soon after the September 11, 2001, terrorist attacks, the United States led an invasion of Afghanistan to oust the Taliban, the ruling regime that was aiding al Qaeda, the terrorist group responsible for the September 11 attacks.

mation of viable, legitimate authority in the country loomed as the two largest postintervention priorities in the region. Hastily convened talks among Afghanistan's competing factions during December in Bonn, Germany, produced a careful, precariously balanced agreement for a transitional government and a postwar future. The bitter rivals in attendance agreed on provisions for emergency and constitutional loya jirgas, an interim power-sharing arrangement, and a schedule for new elections. Over the next 180 days, the United States would lead the coalition effort to continue mopping-up operations in the south of the country while the United Nations would authorize an International Security Assistance Force (ISAF) of five thousand troops to secure Kabul. The emergency loya jirga, ending on June 19, 2002, created the current Afghanistan Interim Administration (AIA). A similar jirga to draft and ratify a new Afghan constitution is to take place by December 2003 and elections for a permanent government are to be held by June 2004.[1]

Cause for Optimism

A year and a half after intervention, the Taliban and al Qaeda are no longer able to mass and stage large-scale attacks. Humanitarian crises are fading. The Afghan government is becoming more coherent over time, and there is now slow movement to develop peace with justice in place of the sense that peace before justice was necessary. Afghans' enthusiasm for participating in defining their future, as witnessed in the loya jirga, is clear. Several delegates,

> *"Postwar security and the formation of viable, legitimate authority in the country loomed as the two largest postintervention priorities."*

11 percent of whom were women, went so far as to tell warlords in attendance that they should not be present. They had blood on their hands, they argued, and Afghanistan deserves better. Delegates still speak of their anger at the closed and secretive process of choosing Afghanistan's president at the loya jirga. This outspokenness is a powerful and remarkable portent of a more hopeful future.

There is additional cause for optimism. Afghanistan has not relapsed into wholesale civil war, no small accomplishment in a country that has known little else for a generation. A pragmatic interim authority was established on schedule. Salaries of most government officials are now being paid, and cash-for-work and food-for-work programs have together created three million jobs. More than two million refugees have returned, a number far exceeding international expectations. The worst humanitarian crises have been contained with food and agricultural assistance, shelter programs, and the improvement of water sources. The rehabilitation of clinics, bazaars, schools, and veterinary cen-

---

1. Afghanistan's new constitution was approved on January 12, 2004, and the interim president, Hamid Karzai, was elected president for a five-year term on October 9, 2004.

ters, along with vaccination and teacher training programs, is under way. Civil liberties have improved. Training of an incipient national army has begun, and in the early months of 2003 international assistance has become more readily available for large-scale repair of roads, communications systems, university facilities, central banking, and government offices. Aid agencies have created an economy unto themselves, with the United States alone spending nearly $350 million in Afghanistan since the end of the war. Violent conflict has exhausted Afghans, and few express much sympathy for war as a useful means to achieve political ends.

Progress Slower than Expected

But progress has also been slower than originally envisioned. The postwar peace remains profoundly vulnerable to the attention-deficit disorder of major donors, growing insecurity in the capital, military feudalism, and the rising impatience of Afghans. The international community has pledged $4.5 billion over five years for reconstruction in Afghanistan. But of the $1.8 billion promised for 2002 at the Tokyo conference in March, only $1 billion has been committed, with even less implemented as assistance in the field. The AIA has claimed that only $560 million in assistance was actually allocated in 2002, of which only $90 million has been given directly to the government to support its operations. Moreover, 80 percent of the total disbursed has funded relief programs rather than reconstruction initiatives. Afghan finance minister Ashraf Ghani has called this a dangerous game, one in which the reluctance and caution that international donors exercise toward the new government and reconstruction may ultimately undermine the fragile peace. Of critical importance to stability, warn Ghani and Afghan president Hamid Karzai, will be the ability of the government in Kabul to become more relevant in the provinces by effectively delivering meaningful reconstruction assistance outside the capital.

Although the AIA is quick to blame the international community for poor performance, the administration lacks the capacity to absorb and manage large amounts of direct assistance or to coordinate the activities of its own interim ministries. Until late August 2002, to the profound frustration of the World Bank and the International Monetary Fund, no financial mechanism existed to channel direct assistance to AIA accounts—the Afghan Central Bank was still busy requesting fax machines, desks, and telephone lines.

> *"Several delegates ... went so far as to tell warlords ... they had blood on their hands ... and Afghanistan deserves better."*

Moreover, only a handful of the Afghan government's twenty-nine ministers are reliable, competent partners with national, rather than regional, vision. The stubborn persistence of humanitarian emergencies in the country has necessitated an international preoccupation with relief programs, and the costs implicit in setting up large assistance operations in unfamiliar territory and in a postwar environment that lacks basic infrastructure mean less net assistance for Afghans.

Further Causes of Delay

Interagency and interpersonal fractiousness in the international community has also been a cause of delay. Literally hundreds of relief and reconstruction strategies exist, some neither coherent nor complementary, among various donor organizations, UN agencies, foreign governments, and international NGOs [nongovernmental organizations]. Lines of authority and communication are ambiguous among the government's own Afghan Assistance Coordination Authority (AACA), its ministries, six UN agencies, the United Nations Assistance Mission in Afghanistan (UNAMA), the ISAF, the Coalition Joint Civil Military Operations Task Force (CJC-MOTF), foreign diplomatic and donor organizations, NGOs, and the new U.S. Provisional Reconstruction Teams (PRTs) to be deployed in the provinces. NGOs are particularly difficult to coordinate. International NGOs, familiar with working in modern postwar environments characterized by weak, corrupt, or nonexistent governments are quick to assert their independence from oversight by the AACA and other coordination bodies. Depending on their source of funding, many organizations participate in coordination efforts to the degree that it suits their interests, and they often deploy according to internal assessments of need, cluster in areas that are easily accessible, or crowd around institutions relevant to their expertise. In the meantime, the conspicuous inequalities of wealth inherent in the operational footprints of aid organizations make Afghans impatient as they wait for the bustle of activity around them to translate into concrete improvements in their daily lives. In addition, a brain drain of overqualified Afghan talent into low-responsibility positions in international agencies continues. The government, now able to pay most of its officials the equivalent of $50 to $75 a month, complains bitterly along with local nongovernmental organizations that they cannot attract or keep good talent as Afghans can earn five to twenty-five times that amount as guards, cooks, drivers, program assistants, and managers for international agencies.

> *Afghans [are] impatient as they wait for the . . . [activities] around them to translate into concrete improvements in their daily lives.*

Also worrisome is the status of refugees who have gravitated to cities where inflation from the aid economy coupled with a scarcity of resources contributes to a rise in urban-rural tensions. Tribalism and more conservative Islamic notions of social and political behavior collide with the relative secularism and urban legal traditions in Afghanistan's cities. There is also a sharpening of exclusive, regional subidentities under way that makes the development of allegiance to Kabul problematic. If this continues, the important advantages the capital may eventually offer in the rule of law, human rights protections, and economic benefits to the provinces will go unrecognized. Of additional concern is the inability of the international community to effectively contain the spread of opium poppy cultivation and the cycles of debt, coercion, and impoverishment it creates. Thus far, largely owing to the dismal failure of last year's [2002] poppy eradication campaign, little assistance has been earmarked by any major donor for a follow-on effort in 2003.

Deteriorating Security Environment

But by far the greatest danger to Afghanistan's stability more than a year after U.S. intervention comes from the worsening security environment. The nine thousand U.S. troops still in Afghanistan have come under increasing fire in the first four months of 2003 from hostile elements based inside Pakistan's western border and in remote parts of Afghanistan. In Kabul, where ISAF maintains a robust presence, assassinations of government officials and an attempt on President Karzai's life, together with explosions in the crowded streets of the city, signal the continuing insecurity of the capital. Outside Kabul, where no international peacekeeping forces are present, powerful warlords and private armies have consolidated their control over much of the rest of the country, increasing the number of human rights violations and lawlessness in the process.

Under the Taliban, the country's endemic military factionalism was weakened. The Taliban's demise and the United States' continuing reliance on warlord proxies to prosecute the war now exaggerate the military feudalism that is reemerging in the postwar power vacuum. Said one U.S. official quoted in the *Washington Post*, "Right now, if you're the enemy of our enemy, you're our friend." The simultaneous execution of a hot war using such surrogates alongside efforts to consolidate postwar peace complicates the U.S. mission in Afghanistan. The strengthening and protection of warlords such as Bacha Khan Zadran, Daoud Khan, Abdul Rashid Dostum, Gul Agha Sherzai, and Ismail Khan to facilitate the fight against terrorism has emboldened many of the same individuals to use their newfound status to more tightly control freedom of movement, to corrupt aid activities, to curtail free expression, and to control market access in their areas.

"By far the greatest danger to Afghanistan's stability . . . comes from the worsening security environment."

These same commanders, many of whom hold civil posts as well, often stand accused of facilitating smuggling, participating in the poppy trade, practicing extortion, and taking part in destructive "green on green" fighting between rival militias and criminal gangs. The percentage of assistance skimmed now, say experienced aid workers, is equal to that stolen during the fighting between the Taliban and the Northern Alliance. U.S. forces disregard the activity and are quick to point out that they are not in Afghanistan to police but to continue the war with al Qaeda. ISAF is of little help. It continues to be confined to Kabul, primarily because of a lack of support from the United States and a lack of will from other nations. The contributions of logistical, intelligence, air evacuation, and backup support that would make ISAF expansion viable have not materialized. With few options, Afghans must still turn to Afghan factional leaders and their irregulars for protection and favors. Some residents, particularly those in areas where corruption is rampant and where skirmishing between warlords is common, are nostalgic for the predictability of life under the Taliban.

Afghanistan Has Made Significant Progress

by Hamid Karzai

About the author: *Hamid Karzai is the president of Afghanistan. During the Soviet occupation from 1979 to 1989, he was active in the Afghan resistance, and in 1992, he became Afghanistan's foreign minister. After the fall of the Taliban regime, Karzai was appointed head of the Interim Administration of Afghanistan and elected interim president by Afghanistan's Loya Jirga (people's assembly) in June 2002. On October 9, 2004, Karzai was elected Afghanistan's president in the country's first general election since the Taliban was ousted in 2001.*

There is no reality more oppressive than the silence of a nation. For too long, Afghanistan was a silenced nation, a country without a voice. After decades of being suppressed to silence, our nation is beginning to have a voice of its own. Recovering from the tragedy of war and destruction, Afghanistan is determined to reverse the effects of the suffering it has long endured.

A lot has changed in Afghanistan over the last two years from 2001 to 2003. But no change is so critical and pervasive than the animated response from the people of Afghanistan to the recent developments in our country. I find no sight more rewarding than the sight of our young girls and boys flocking to schools every morning; I find few things more engaging than the company of elderly representatives who come to Kabul from far-flung provinces of the country to discuss their priorities for reconstruction; and, in the same order, there is nothing more enthusing than the active participation of Afghan men and women in the process of public consultation for the new constitution.

The people of Afghanistan, we know from the public consultation conducted in connection with the constitution drafting process, want a modern unitary state that is committed to Islamic values and the preservation of peace and national unity. A state that insures security for all its citizens, enforces justice and the rule of law, and promotes prosperity. Like any post-war society, the need for security and removing the threat of arms and armed factions is a compelling issue for all Afghans. Our people demand the establishment of truly national and

Hamid Karzai, address to the 58th Session of the General Assembly of the United Nations, New York, September 23, 2003.

competent institutions, notably the Army and the Police. Afghans want state institutions that are professional and representative; and an administration that is efficient and free of corruption. The Afghan people want tolerance for other religions, protection of human rights, and affirmative actions to promote the rights of women.

Since I addressed [the General Assembly of the United Nations] in September of last year [2002], Afghanistan has taken significant strides in the path of postwar reconstruction. While total stability may not have been achieved yet, Afghanistan today is more stable and peaceful than at any other period in its recent history. The International Security Assistance Force (ISAF), to the credit of the participating countries, has done a tremendous job of securing the nation's capital. This is partly the reason that people from other parts of the country have demanded that ISAF be expanded to their areas too. We see the NATO's [North Atlantic Treaty Organization] decision to take over the command of ISAF in Kabul as a positive development. The Afghan people have also welcomed the Provincial Reconstruction Teams (PRTs)[1] that are supported by the coalition member states. Reconstruction and security are tied together, and we are absolutely certain that, no matter what flag they fly, forces that ensure stability will be welcomed throughout Afghanistan.

> *"Afghanistan today is more stable and peaceful than at any other period in its recent history."*

Afghanistan's Achievements

We recognize, however, that providing security to the people of Afghanistan is ultimately our own responsibility. We are grateful to the international community, the United States and Germany in particular, for making a determined effort to help us embark on a process of reforming and rebuilding our security institutions, namely the Afghan National Army and the National Police. After an arduous process of restructuring, we have just completed the Reform of the Ministry of Defense. This step is now paving the way for the implementation of the nation-wide programme on Disarmament, Demobilisation and Re-integration (DDR) which will begin in earnest in mid October [2003] with assistance from Japan.

Constitution is the bedrock of the modern state. Under the Bonn Agreement, my government was assigned the historic task of giving Afghanistan its new constitution. After a broad process of consultation, the commission assigned to the task has just finished the draft constitution. The draft will be submitted for approval to a Constitutional Loya Jirga, or Afghan Grand Council, in Decem-

---

1. Provincial Reconstruction Teams (PRTs) are groups of fifty to one hundred military personnel sent to establish security and begin reconstruction projects in the provinces of Afghanistan.

ber. Work on the reform of the judicial system, and on drafting of new secondary laws, has also been continuing with notable outcomes achieved in recent months. The Political Parties Law and the Banking Law have now been officially adopted.

Having started from a below-zero baseline, the 30 percent economic growth rate which Afghanistan enjoyed last year is a promising start. Committed as we are to an open market economy, and seeing the private sector as the true engine for growth, we have moved aggressively to create the legal and financial frameworks for a positive environment to the private sector. Our newly adopted laws that govern investment, banking and property rights, the new stable currency, and the bureaucratic reforms we have enacted, provide a liberal and conducive underpinning to a rapid economic growth. Like never before, Afghanistan is open to business. Once in the past, Afghanistan was at the center of a global [terrorist] threat. Our vision for the future is that Afghanistan should be a center for economic opportunity. We do not call ourselves a landlocked country, we are rather a land-bridging country. Afghanistan connects together South Asia, Central Asia and the Middle East, a fact to which geo-strategists have long been attracted. But it is time that Afghanistan's vast potential for facilitating trade and economic activity is exploited.

Education and Narcotics Programs

Through such nation-wide programmes as the National Solidarity Programme (NSP) the Government aims to take reconstruction to the villages and households of Afghanistan. Perhaps no other priority features more widely in the demands of the Afghan people than the provision of education. Today, almost 40 percent of the students and teachers in primary and secondary education are female. This is a huge rise from the close to zero percentage that we inherited from the Taliban. Millions of text books have been published, and schools are being built at a higher pace than ever. However, like in other areas of service provision, the need is much greater than our capacity to deliver.

> *"As we acknowledge that the road ahead . . . is long and tortuous, we appreciate that significant achievements have been made over the last two years."*

The struggle against production and trafficking of narcotics continues. We see a direct connection between narcotics and terrorism, and it is in our absolute national interest to fight both. Both are transnational challenges. We in the region and in the international community must make the strategic decision, in the spirit of true partnership, to fight against both menaces.

As we acknowledge that the road ahead of Afghanistan is long and tortuous, we appreciate that significant achievements have been made over the last two years.

The New Constitution Is Proof of Political Progress in Afghanistan

by Zalmay Khalilzad

About the author: *Former Afghan national Zalmay Khalilzad is the U.S. ambassador and special presidential envoy to Afghanistan. His published works include* Prospects of the Interim Afghan Government *and* From Containment to Global Leadership? America and the World After the Cold War.

The constitutional loya jirga [people's assembly] that concluded in Kabul Sunday [January 4, 2004] was a milestone on the Afghan people's path to democracy. Afghans have seized the opportunity provided by the United States and its international partners to lay the foundation for democratic institutions and provide a framework for national elections in 2004.

The Afghan people manifested this remarkable commitment to democracy in two ways. They defied the enemies of Afghanistan's progress—remnants of the extremist Taliban and al Qaeda forces[1]—by participating in elections for the delegates to the constitutional loya jirga. The extremists sought to intimidate candidates and voters. They failed.

Women especially were not intimidated. There was a powerful reversal of symbolism when the Kabul soccer stadium—used less than three years ago by the Taliban to execute women accused of adultery—was used by thousands of women to choose their representatives to the constitutional loya jirga. Of the voting delegates, 102 were women—more than 20 percent of the total delegates.

Second, Afghans overcame their past. Instead of relying on the power of the gun, they embraced the often difficult and sometimes messy democratic process of debating, listening and compromising. They trusted in the power of their

---

1. Afghanistan's former rulers, the Taliban, aided al Qaeda, the terrorist group responsible for the September 11, 2001, terrorist attacks.

words by openly deliberating the important issues. Afghans used newspapers, radios, teahouses, schools, universities, mosques—even the Internet—as forums to debate fundamental issues such as the system of government, the role of religion, human rights—particularly the role of women—and, in a country with more than a dozen ethnic groups, such emotional issues as official languages and the relationship between the center and provinces. Such a wide-ranging debate is unprecedented in more than 5,000 years of Afghan history.

An Enlightened Islamic Constitution

The Afghan people's desire to succeed overcame the potential for failure. In the midst of sharp debates, the delegates and people of Afghanistan were unswervingly committed to obtaining a sound constitution. Attempts by warlords and religious fundamentalists to hijack the process were thwarted. Women and minorities held leadership roles. When one brave young woman denounced some of the delegates for their role in the destruction of Afghanistan in the 1990s, the chairman initially sought to throw her out of the hall. The delegates

> *"With the Afghan people and the world watching . . . [Afghanistan] adopted one of the most enlightened constitutions in the Islamic world."*

forced him to relent, and Malalai Joya refused to be intimidated and went on to play an active role in her working committee. By the loya jirga's completion, three women were part of the seven-member leadership team and several more took leading positions in the working committees. When ethnic and regional divisions emerged as possible fault lines over issues such as official languages, the delegates decided to find unity in diversity by making all languages official where they are spoken by the majority. This is unprecedented for Afghanistan and the region. With the Afghan people and the world watching, Hazares, Pashtuns, Tajiks, Turkmen, Uzbeks and others [Afghanistan's ethnic groups] adopted one of the most enlightened constitutions in the Islamic world.

The Afghan constitution sets forth a presidential system with a strong parliament and an independent judiciary. The final document embraces a centralized government structure, which reflects most delegates' belief that years of war and the destruction of national institutions have left the central government far too weak. Delegates strengthened parliament by determining basic state policies and requiring confirmation of key presidential appointees, including the head of the central bank and the director of the national intelligence service.

The Afghan constitution also sets forth parallel commitments to Islam and to human rights. While embracing Islam as the state religion, the document provides broad religious freedom—allowing adherents of other faiths to practice their religions and observe religious rites. The loya jirga increased the number of women in parliament to an average of two female representatives from each province and explicitly stated, "Citizens of Afghanistan—whether men or women—have rights and duties before the law." Accepting equality between men and women marks a revolutionary change in the roles women are able to play in Afghan government and society.

Investing in Success

The United Nations has played a vital role in building Afghan political institutions since the Bonn Conference set the country on its current course. In particular the secretary general's special representative, Lakhdar Brahimi, was critical in helping the loya jirga delegates bridge their differences and achieve this successful outcome.

Afghanistan faces more challenges: implementing this constitution, defeating the remaining extremists and terrorists, disarming militias, strengthening national institutions, eliminating narcotics production and helping the poorest of Afghans gain a foothold on the ladder of opportunity. After the suffering of the past 20 years, ordinary people of Afghanistan want their country to work. By adopting a sound constitution through an orderly and transparent process, Afghans have cleared a major hurdle.

Afghanistan has sent a compelling message to the rest of the world that by investing in that country's development, the United States is investing in success. Americans can take pride in the role we have played in leading the multilateral effort to support Afghan democratization. The toppling of the Taliban and the stabilizing presence of the coalition and NATO [North Atlantic Treaty Organization] International Security Assistance Force troops have enabled the seeds of political progress to sprout. President [George W.] Bush's decision to increase aid to Afghanistan—which will likely total more than $2 billion in fiscal 2004—will accelerate reconstruction of the country's national army, police force, economic infrastructure, schools and medical system.

> *"Afghanistan has sent a compelling message to the . . . world that by investing in that country's development, the United States is investing in success."*

Our work in Afghanistan is not yet done. It will take several years and a sustained commitment of significant resources by the United States and the international community before the country can stand on its own feet. Given the stakes involved, we must remain committed for as long as it takes to succeed.

Optimism for Progress in Afghanistan Is Warranted

by the *Economist*

About the author: *The* Economist *is a weekly magazine featuring economic and political analyses of U.S. and world events.*

Afghanistan is starting to get a few things right. But outsiders still need to do much more.

As in Iraq, good news has been in short supply in Afghanistan. A spate of attacks on aid workers has made much of the country's south a no-go area for relief, let alone reconstruction efforts. Last week [in November 2003], the United Nations gave warning that opium production has risen in the past year, to levels exceeding those seen before the Taliban brutally enforced a ban on the crop. Skirmishing between rival warlords continues in the supposedly peaceful north, even while America's forces along the border with Pakistan have been coming under fierce attacks from Taliban and al-Qaeda [terrorist group] remnants there. It is increasingly tempting to write off the American-led coalition's adventure in Afghanistan as a costly mistake, and to despair of rescuing that blighted land from the cycle of failure and war that has been its lot for a quarter of century.

Grounds for Optimism

Tempting, but wrong. Those inclined to see glasses as half-full rather than half-empty can point to some grounds for qualified optimism. One is the publication this week [November 2003], only slightly delayed, of a draft constitution for Afghanistan, likely to be approved next month. The draft has much to recommend it. By declaring Afghanistan an Islamic republic whose law will conform with Islamic precepts, but not impose them slavishly, it appears to have bridged a gap between the country's modernisers and the traditionalists who wanted full-blown sharia law, stonings and all. The constitution vests most authority in an elected president whose powers will not, as was once proposed, be checked by a prime minister. In principle, this might produce an over-strong leader at the centre but could produce effective government if the conciliatory incumbent, Hamid Karzai, gets the job.[1]

There are other reasons for hope. Gradually, Mr Karzai has started to assert the role of the centre against the regional commanders. He has already persuaded them to start paying taxes to Kabul [the government seat] (though the amount will surely be modest), and has replaced the governors of Kandahar and Gardez. The warlords of the north, Rashid Dostum and Atta Mohammed, have been summoned to jobs in Kabul—though it is still far from clear that they will heed the summons without some vigorous

> *"It is . . . tempting to write off the American-led coalition's adventure in Afghanistan as a costly mistake. . . . Tempting, but wrong."*

American arm-twisting. A national army, which has a vital role to play in employing the young men who currently serve Afghanistan's numerous private armies, is starting to take shape. The $287 [million] earmarked for it in the Iraq-Afghanistan appropriation approved by the American Senate . . . could make a significant impact. And all the while, in areas like Kabul and Herat that are relatively safe, the economy is slowly starting to revive. Compared with the repression of the Taliban, or the appalling slaughter of the early 1990s, the fortunes of much of Afghanistan are greatly improved.

Recovery Is Fragile

All this is evidence that Afghans can indeed help themselves, if only they are given a chance. But the recovery, such as it is, is fragile. Outsiders can do much more to help it along, especially now that America has stopped insisting dogmatically that it is not in the business of "nation-building".

Pay up, or watch this state fail again.

Money is the foremost requirement. Afghanistan has been treated less generously than other post-conflict states, such as East Timor, Bosnia and now Iraq. The American Congress . . . allocated $18.6 billion for rebuilding Iraq, but only $1.2 billion for Afghanistan, even though Afghanistan has more people, more pressing needs and fewer resources of its own (apricots, not oil). Other pledges amount to only $4.5 billion over five years. This is not nearly enough. Until roads are rebuilt and the smashed irrigation system repaired, Afghan farmers have no real option but to grow opium, with baleful consequences for both internal politics and the outside world.

As in Iraq, however, money is hard to spend effectively in an atmosphere of lawlessness and violence. And though NATO [North Atlantic Treaty Organization] has taken over command of ISAF [International Security Assistance

---

1. On October 9, 2004, Hamid Karzai was elected president of Afghanistan in the country's first general election since the Taliban was ousted in 2001.

Force], Afghanistan's tiny peacekeeping force, it has not tried hard enough to extend its remit beyond Kabul. To be effective, more outside troops are needed, together with a greater willingness to use them to face down the warlords, some of whom have bigger barks than bites. Finally, the country needs to arrive at a fairer distribution of political power. By helping America in the war, the Tajik minority ended up with too much control. This undermines Mr Karzai's authority among his own frustrated Pushtun majority, the very group from which the Taliban regime drew its core support. But once a constitution is in hand, the way will be open for a nationwide election that should in due course help redress the balance.

Economic Progress and Security Are Evident in Postwar Afghanistan

by John Jennings

About the author: *John Jennings is a journalist and commentator who has written extensively on Afghanistan for the Associated Press, the* Economist, *and the* Washington Times. *He has also worked as a Dari interpreter for the BBC.*

Since the overthrow of the Taliban, most media reports on Afghanistan have warned of rising lawlessness throughout the countryside. Outside the capital Kabul, which is patrolled by International peacekeeping troops, we are told that "anarchy" prevails. The reports attribute this state of affairs to America's military alliance with provincial "warlords." These regional and local leaders—mostly mujahideen [Islamic warriors], veterans of the 1980s jihad against the Soviet occupation army and its Afghan client regime—are portrayed as incessantly feuding robber barons, whose armed bands routinely exploit their relationship with the Pentagon to brutalize the populace.

The country is "sliding back into chaos, poverty and despair," *Newsweek* insisted on September 8 [2003]. The BBC, quoting a letter to British Foreign Secretary Jack Straw from several private charities active in Afghanistan, reported on August 10 that "large swaths" of Afghanistan "are under the control of warlords where people live daily under the threat of violence." On May 6, UN [United Nation] envoy Lakhdar Brahimi insisted the security issue "casts a long shadow over . . . the whole future of Afghanistan." That remark contradicted U.S. defense secretary Donald Rumsfeld's May 1 claim that "the bulk of [Afghanistan] is permissive and secure."

But in fact, Rumsfeld was right, as I ascertained during a September visit. Claims of widespread and deteriorating security are simply not true.

John Jennings, "Assessing the Myth of Disarray," *Terrorism Monitor*, vol. 1, November 20, 2003.

Chapter 1

The Countryside Is Peaceful

During my travels, I concentrated on populous areas under the sway of anti-Taliban leaders, since it is here that U.S. policy is most often said to have failed. I visited three of the country's five largest cities—Kabul [the capital], Mazar-e Sharif [in north Afghanistan] and Jalalabad [in east Afghanistan]—and the countryside around each, with side trips to the Panjsher Valley and to the Pakistan border. I traveled overland, on public transport, unarmed, unaccompanied, and among ordinary Afghans, querying them about conditions near their homes and along the highways. I haunted bazaars and teahouses, interrogating fellow patrons and the staff.

The highways are wide open, the cities calm. With very few, localized exceptions, the countryside is at peace. Checkpoints run by renegade gunmen are notably absent, so food and fuel are cheap. More goods and passengers are moving farther and more freely than they have in decades. These are sensitive indicators of good local security and nationwide economic recovery. It's clear the so-called "warlords" are not running amok. If they were, extortionate roadblocks on the main highways would be the first sign of it since that is where the money is. Transit trade is a pillar of the Afghan economy.

Afghan visitors and Herat residents alike give regional leader Ismail Khan particular praise for maintaining security and protecting commerce. Truck and bus drivers plying the Kabul-Kandahar-Herat road say that highway robberies, their main concern, are relatively rare. I met a Panjsheri driver for a transport cartel who had recently traveled to Herat via Kandahar, then driven back a new vehicle: a journey unthinkable for a northerner before the U.S. intervention. The biggest health hazards on Afghan highways today are drivers passing on blind curves and the unprecedented clouds of dust and diesel fumes.

Exceptions to Good Security Are Rare

Granted, there are exceptions, such as a recent outbreak of fighting near Mazar-e-Sharif [in northern Afghanistan]. But rare instances such as this help to prove the rule that ordinary Afghans—at least the majority living in areas not contested by terrorist remnants—have it better today than at any time since 1978.

In the mountainous, sparsely populated area along the southeastern border, Pakistan-based Taliban fighters this year [2003] intensified their campaign of small scale raids targeting both coalition troops and their Afghan allies. Some reports credit them with having seized a handful of remote district headquarters on the border. But they have neither closed major roads nor besieged large towns—historically easy tasks even for marginal Afghan factions, thanks to foreign backing and the country's fragmented politics and tortuous ge-

> *"Claims of widespread and deteriorating security are simply not true."*

ography. Despite retaining such advantages, plus a relatively small U.S. troop presence and plentiful local collaborators (most of whom simply trimmed their beards and went home when the Taliban regime was overthrown), the purportedly resurgent Taliban have yet to make much headway.

Outside the border region, disgruntled ex-Taliban occasionally attack [President Hamid] Karzai officials, aid workers and international peace keepers. But aside from a handful of terrorist attacks in Kabul itself, this threat is limited overwhelmingly to the former Taliban heartland.

Security Issue Is Exaggerated

Afghan and foreign critics alike told me that aid workers, particularly UN officials, have exaggerated the security issue. One Kabul-based expatriate and longtime observer argued, "A disproportionate number of aid workers and media types have been so dulled by Western society that they lack the 'edge' necessary to do their job. . . . [They] are ill-informed simply because they are increasingly afraid to take the risks inherent in completing their research." A Western military officer rolled his eyes over opposition to military-led Provincial Reconstruction Teams[1] based on the argument the PRTs blur the distinction between humanitarian and military activities. The officer speculated that the real objection was fear of being upstaged by military engineers and medics, who unlike many civilian aid workers, will not flee at the first rumor of unrest.

> *"Ordinary Afghans—at least the majority living in areas not contested by terrorist remnants—have it better today than at any time since 1978."*

Dozens of other foreigners also ignored reports of supposed widespread instability. While I was in Afghanistan, thirty-odd British trekkers left on a 100-km hike up the Panjsher Valley northeast of Kabul. Then I met Mariko, a Japanese travel agent who had just returned from leading a group of seven tourists on a two-week jeep trip through Afghanistan's central highlands. While there, here party met yet another band of foreigners. They were traveling in a vehicle bearing the distinctive logo of a Western "humanitarian" agency, driven by an Afghan employee of same who was moonlighting as a tour guide. Mariko and I joked that the driver probably explained his absence by claiming the local "warlord" had held him hostage.

Mariko had first visited Afghanistan in June [2003] to verify security conditions firsthand. Yet, just as she decided the situation was good, UN special envoy Lakhdar Brahimi warned that security was so bad that the UN might not be able to supervise next year's elections.

---

1. PRTs are teams of fifty to one hundred U.S. and coalition military personnel dispatched to the provinces to establish peace and begin reconstruction projects.

The Taliban's Resurgence Threatens Afghanistan's Reconstruction

by Phil Zabriskie

About the author: *Phil Zabriskie is a journalist from New York City who lives in Asia and works as a correspondent for* TimeAsia *magazine. He has written extensively on Afghanistan, Iraq, and events in south, east, and Southeast Asia.*

In the mountains of Afghanistan, summer is the season for fighting. The past three months [July–September 2003] have seen more than their usual share of it as remnants of the Taliban [Islamic fundamentalist former rulers of Afghanistan], ousted from power by U.S. and coalition forces in 2001, have regrouped, attacked remote government outposts, held positions for a few days—and then, usually, vanished at the first whup-whup of approaching U.S. Blackhawk helicopters. Not last week [September 2003]. After ambushing a small garrison in Zabul province [in southeast Afghanistan], several hundred Taliban fighters hid in a needle-thin gorge known as Moray Pass, waiting to attack U.S. troops and their Afghan allies. Shielded by overhanging rock, the Taliban were protected from U.S. bombers and helicopters, and fighting raged for several days. Local villagers reported seeing Taliban fighters scrambling up the hillside carrying their dead and wounded. Zabul's provincial governor, Hafizullah Hashami, said 40 Talibs were killed and several coalition soldiers wounded. Later the Pentagon said one American special-operations soldier died after falling during a night attack. It would be tempting to say the Taliban is back, were the evidence not all too clear that it never went very far away. While the world's attention has been fixed on Iraq, the other war has sparked back into life. Having nursed themselves back to health in Pakistan, Taliban forces are re-energized and determined to avenge their defeat. The Taliban's old structures may still be largely intact; a Kabul-based security official says the "neo-Taliban" is guided by many of the same men who ran Afghanistan's theocracy from 1996 through 2001, when it provided protection for Osama bin Laden [the terrorist leader who allegedly masterminded the September 11, 2001, attacks on the United States] and the terrorist camps of al-Qaeda. General Garni, military commander of Zabul, speculated last week that Mullah Mohammed Omar, the Taliban's one-eyed Commander of the Faithful, might be hiding in the province's mountains with 800 men. The Taliban has deepened its alliance with warlord Gulbuddin Hekmatyar and his fundamentalist, anti-Western Hizb-i-Islami Party, which remains potent in eastern Afghanistan. Hekmatyar used to have close ties to Iran, and Pakistani sympathizers of the Taliban say Tehran may be secretly bankrolling the rebels to tie down U.S. troops in Afghanistan.

Washington has noticed the deteriorating situation. "Clashes with the Taliban are up," says a State Department official. "It's not sweetness and light. You've got warlordism, banditry, fighting. Those are serious problems." In response, the Administration is finalizing a plan to double its aid to Afghanistan, now running at around $1 billion annually.

Afghanistan would not be such a worry if Taliban fighters were not able to find a haven in Pakistan among fellow ethnic Pashtuns [the dominant ethnic group in Afghanistan]. With their beards trimmed and often without their trademark black turbans, they blend in easily. In the Pakistani town of Quetta, as in the border village of Chaman, pro-Taliban graffiti are common and copies of recordings made by Mullah Omar are available in the marketplace. Standing in the middle of a bustling street in Quetta, Aghar Jan, who fled Afghanistan in 2001, loudly proclaims his willingness to take up Omar's call to jihad and expel the "infidels" now in charge. "I'm waiting for the order of the emir," he says, referring to Omar. "When the order comes," he says, "I'm ready to carry out a suicide attack."

That's not an idle boast. A year ago, says Massood Khalili, a senior member of the anti-Taliban Northern Alliance now serving as ambassador to India, "the Taliban were scared, broken and disconcerted." But now, he says, they have re-emerged "slowly, gradually, like a photograph developing." The Taliban, says General Mohammed Akram, until recently police chief of Afghanistan's Kandahar province, are "stronger now than at any time since the fall of their government." They are certainly more adventurous. In July and August [2003], Taliban gunmen briefly took over government offices in Zabul and Paktika provinces. Raiding parties

> *"It would be tempting to say the Taliban is back, were the evidence not all too clear that it never went very far away."*

from Pakistan can consist of hundreds of well-armed troops. They try to avoid U.S. military patrols, instead targeting Afghan soldiers and policemen. Aid workers and anyone else deemed to support the U.S. or Afghan President Hamid Karzai, including civilians and religious officials, are also fair game. Four anti-Taliban mullahs in the Kandahar area have been assassinated in the past two months, and 15 people, including six children, died on Aug. 13 [2003], when the bus they were riding was bombed in Helmand province.

In Afghanistan the blame for the Taliban's revival is laid firmly at [the Pakistan capital of] Islamabad's door. Pakistani authorities have arrested roughly 500 suspected al-Qaeda members, but Karzai has charged that Pakistan shows little inclination to apprehend top-level Talibs. "If we had sincere and honest cooperation from Pakistan," declares a security official in Kabul, "there'd be no Taliban threat in Afghanistan." Faisal Saleh Hayat, Pakistan's Interior Minister, insists that "our focus is equally on al-Qaeda and on the Taliban." But despite public pronouncements of gratitude to Pakistan, the U.S.'s ally in the global war on terrorism, some U.S. officials are growing increasingly frustrated at Islamabad's performance. Says a State Department official: "Even the Saudis are doing better than Pakistan in countering al-Qaeda. The only thing Pakistan does is skim 10% off the top of the al-Qaeda presence when we complain."

> *"Taliban cells have been established and charged with specific responsibilities, such as bombings, . . . burning schools down, . . . [and] targeting foreigners."*

The margin decreases when it comes to the Taliban. A Pakistani intelligence operative stationed near Chaman says his orders are "not to harass or appease" the Taliban but to let them be. Pakistan's border provinces are controlled by Jamiat Ulema Islam, an extremist Islamic party, and Afghan intelligence officials claim that provincial ministers in Baluchistan help the Talibs find safe houses. "We feel much safer now," a commander told *Time* in Peshawar. In Quetta, a local cleric says Taliban commanders meet openly and regularly to plan raids into their former domain.

Mullah Omar is believed to have spent the summer moving throughout southwestern Afghanistan. According to Taliban spokesman Mohammed Mukhtar Mujahid, Omar has formed a 10-man leadership council and assigned each lieutenant a region to destabilize. This guerrilla war cabinet includes Mullah Dadullah Akhund, a one-legged intelligence chief who in March ordered the execution of a Salvadorean Red Cross worker in Uruzgan province, and several top leaders. A Taliban field commander tells *Time* that Taliban cells have been established and charged with specific responsibilities, such as bombings, preventing children from going to school or burning schools down, attacking government troops, assassinating progovernment mullahs, targeting foreigners and propaganda. Funding is believed to come from Pakistan, some Arab countries and al-Qaeda. Mullah Nik Mohammed, a Taliban commander captured in Spin Boldak, told his interrogators in June that he would have received $850 for detonating a bomb, double that if it killed a civilian, and $2,600 for taking a soldier's life.

For Rohan Gunaratna, a Singapore-based expert on al-Qaeda, the Taliban's revival spells trouble beyond the region. "Al-Qaeda is able to survive because of its link with the Taliban," says Gunaratna, arguing that a group of foreigners could not stay in Baluchistan and the North-West Frontier province if the Taliban did not vouch for them. In this view, the Taliban is still harboring al-Qaeda—not, as formerly, in Afghanistan but in Pakistan. And al-Qaeda fighters may be joining with the Taliban in operations. A spokesman for Karzai insisted that Pakistanis and Arabs were part of the raiding party that killed seven Afghan policemen in Paktika province on Aug. 17 [2003].

On top of a ruined economy, continued banditry and the return of the opium trade, a revived Taliban is the last thing that Karzai's poor nation needs. In a speech last month on Afghanistan's Independence Day, Karzai said, "It is the duty of everybody to launch a holy war to reconstruct this nation." The Taliban has already launched a holy war of its own. Soon enough the snows will come and the summer's fighting will die down. But if the U.S. and its ally Pakistan do not crush the Taliban soon, next year promises more bloodshed. "We are waiting," says Qari Rehman, a Talib in Chaman. "You will see. The situation will get worse."

Afghan Warlords Are Undermining Democracy in Afghanistan

by Omar Zakhilwal

About the author: *Omar Zakhilwal is a member of Afghanistan's Loya Jirga (people's assembly) and a board member of the Institute for Afghan Studies, an organization of Afghan scholars designed to promote a better understanding of Afghan affairs through research and commentary.*

I am a member of the Loya Jirga's [Afghanistan's people's assembly] silent majority—or rather, silenced majority—who came to Kabul expecting to shape our nation's future but instead find ourselves being dragged back into the past.

We came from all parts of the country to claim our freedom and democracy, but instead are being met with systematic threats and intimidation aimed at undermining our free choice. We came strengthened by international declarations on human rights, but instead are facing international complicity in the denial of our rights. We came to represent the diverse interests of the entire Afghan nation, 1,500 delegates for 25 million people, but instead are being pressured to support the narrow agenda of warlords and their foreign sponsors. We came to inaugurate an inclusive and professional transitional government, but instead are being compelled to rubberstamp the Bonn Agreement's[1] injust power-sharing arrangements.

The fundamental question we face is this: will the new government be dominated by the same warlords and factional politics responsible for two decades of violence and impunity, or can we break with this legacy and begin to establish a system of law and professional governance?

The Afghan people have spoken clearly on this issue. I recently participated

---

1. The Bonn Agreement was signed in 2001 in Bonn, Germany, between Afghanistan and the international community. It set out a political and reconstruction agenda for Afghanistan.

in a UN-commissioned assessment mission by the Center for Economic and Social Rights, a human rights group based in New York. Our report documents widespread agreement among all Afghans, from urban professionals to landless farmers, that there should be no role for warlords in the country's future, and that international aid will be wasted unless the underlying conditions of peace and security are first established.

The same consensus holds in the Loya Jirga. I estimate that at least 80% of delegates favor excluding all warlords from the government. The 200 women delegates are especially outspoken on this issue. In a spontaneous display of democracy, they publicly rebuked two powerful symbols of Afghanistan's violent past—Burhannudin Rabbani, former President of the Mujahideen [warlord] government from 1992–96, and Gen. Mohammed Fahim, former intelligence chief during this period and currently Defense Minister in the interim government.

Warlords Gain Control

But due to behind-the-scenes pressure, our voices are being silenced and the warlords empowered. Let me give some concrete examples.

When the Loya Jirga opened, support for former King Zahir Shah was extremely strong. Rather than address the issue democratically, almost two days of the six-day Loya Jirga were wasted while a parade of high-level officials from the interim government, the United Nations, and the United States visited Zahir Shah and eventually "persuaded" him to publicly renounce his political ambitions.

> *"[We] came to Kabul expecting to shape our nation's future but instead find ourselves being dragged back into the past."*

When the Loya Jirga recommenced, the delegates were surprised to see Afghanistan's thirty provincial governors, none of whom were elected to serve in the grand assembly. It soon became apparent that their purpose was to serve as arm-twisters for the interim government, which dominated by warlords from the Northern Alliance.[2] "You are all with me. You will do as I tell you to do. If you dare not to follow me we all go back to our province after this [Loya Jirga], don't we?", is a direct quote from a governor to the delegates of his province.

These men controlled less than 10% of the country before the fall of the Taliban, and therefore have little direct influence over most Loya Jirga members, especially those from rural areas in the South, East and West. The governors, on the other hand, are able to leverage their local military and financial power to pressure delegates from their provinces to support handpicked candidates allied to the Northern Alliance. Their persuasive abilities are enhanced by scores of Interior Ministry agents who are circulating throughout the Loya Jirga com-

2. The Northern Alliance is a group of warlords from north Afghanistan that has received support from the United States. It fought against the Taliban during the 2001 war.

pound and openly intimidating outspoken delegates.

Equally discouraging is the role played by the involved international organizations and the expectations set forth by them. An adviser to UN [United Nations] chief Lakhdar Brahimi told me in no uncertain terms that the Loya Jirga was not aimed to bring about fundamental political changes like ridding the government of warlords. Meanwhile, Zalmay Khalilzad, US Special Envoy on Afghanistan, has caused some disappointment in the Loya Jirga through pressure tactics aimed at undercutting popular support for Zahir Shah.

Representatives Are Demoralized

The Loya Jirga is being treated as a ratification tool for backroom political deals. As one example, the media has reported on the "voluntary" decision of Interior Minister Yunus Qanooni to drop his candidacy. But it is not being reported that he will assume an equally powerful post in the new government, or that his intended replacement is himself a member of Qanooni's Northern Alliance faction (as is Fahim and Foreign Minister Abdullah Abdullah).

On the first day of the Loya Jirga, we were filled with hope and enthusiasm. Most of us stayed up past midnight in spirited debates about the country's future. By the third day, a palpable demoralization has set in. Our time is being wasted on trivial procedural matters. We feel manipulated and harassed. Our historic responsibility to the Afghan nation is becoming a charade.

We are in Kabul because we believe that participation and democracy are more than words on paper. We are not asking for much, after all. Simply the right to determine our own government and future in accordance with the human rights ideals so loudly trumpeted by the international community. The same rights as all other people.

Afghanistan's New Constitution Is Flawed

by Amin Tarzi

About the author: *Amin Tarzi is a senior research associate at the Monterey Institute of International Studies in San Francisco specializing in Afghanistan and Iraq affairs. He is an American citizen of Afghan origin and a former U.S. marine.*

On 26 January [2004] Afghan Transitional Administration Chairman [and Afghan president] Hamid Karzai signed into law the new Constitution of the Islamic Republic of Afghanistan. Present at the signing ceremonies and sitting next to Karzai was the frail former monarch of Afghanistan, Mohammad Zaher, who had some 40 years earlier in 1964 signed his own constitution for the country.

Those members of the international community that have backed the process of Afghanistan's emergence from years of foreign intervention, civil war, and despotic rulers have rightfully welcomed the new Afghan Constitution as a guideline with which the country can reemerge as nation-state.

Strictly from a textual point of view, the new Afghan Constitution represents a good starting point for the country on its path of forming a pluralistic and inclusive society in which, in due time, true democracy can be fostered. However, as the history of constitutionalism in Afghanistan sadly illustrates, the texts of most of the six previous constitutions that have been promulgated did not truly reflect the aspirations of the majority of the people of Afghanistan. It can be argued that most of the previous constitutions, to varying degrees, were drafted and passed without much input from the Afghan masses. Thus, constitutions of the past fell victim to intrigues and manipulations of various centers of power that viewed those constitutions as threats to their status in the society.

Claims of Foul Play

Two days after the adoption of the new constitution, a group of around 20 delegates to the Loya Jirga [people's assembly] headed by Abdul Hafez Mansur, claimed that the document signed into law by Karzai does not exactly conform to the draft agreed upon by the Loya Jirga. Mansur, a member of the religiously conservative Jamiat-e Islami and one of the staunchest supporters of a parliamentary system, said that "the constitution which was signed by [Karzai], if it is carefully read . . . compared to the constitution approved and ratified by delegates to the Loya Jirga has changes."

Mansur claimed to have personally "discovered more than 15 changes."

The Constitutional Commission rejected Mansur's charges, stating that some misunderstandings may have occurred, due to the fact that delegates to the Loya Jirga were handed a draft of the constitution on the night

> *"Constitutions of the past fell victim to intrigues and manipulations of various centers of power that viewed those constitutions as threats to their status in the society."*

of 3 January [2004] before the assembly made final changes to the document. Kabir Ranjbar, head of Afghan Lawyers Association, said on 29 January that while the draft of the constitution approved by the Loya Jirga, has indeed been altered, these "changes do not affect the content of the constitution and are not something to be taken seriously." Ranjbar suggested that people "should not discredit the document or lessen the interest of the people regarding the document and regarding its enforcement."

While Ranjbar's suggestion that people ought to regard the new Afghan Constitution as a whole as a good framework for Afghanistan to move ahead is valid and ought to be heeded, the history of the country has illustrated that even constitutions that were formulated with the good of the nation in mind, were forward-looking, and were approved in appropriate fashion became tools for the dissenters, who sought to derail the overall process of state building. As such, the wording of the new Afghan Constitution should leave no room for misunderstanding, and the process through which it was adopted should have been very transparent. Any lingering opacity or perception of foul play about the constitution will make the already difficult task of implementation an even thornier undertaking.

Controversies over the Role of Islam

Commenting on the draft of the Afghan Constitution, I wrote in November [2003]: "The most dangerous legislation here regarding the role of religion remains Article 3 . . . because it might easily be used by conservative religious forces to undermine legislators that they deem to be 'un-Islamic.' The interpretation of which laws might be 'contrary to . . . Islam' is an open-ended proposition that is not immune to abuse." Article 3 of the draft constitution stipulated that "no law can be contrary to the sacred religion of Islam" and the values enshrined in the constitution. In the approved version of the constitution, Article 3 was amended to read, "In Afghanistan, no law can be contrary to the beliefs and provisions of the sacred religion of Islam." Omitted in the final text is the reference to the values enshrined in the constitution.

Even before Hamid Karzai signed the new constitution into law, controversy over the vagueness of Article 3 sparked controversy between the conservative Islamists and the more moderate, secular-oriented forces in Afghanistan.

The controversy began when the state-owned Afghanistan Television surprised its prime-time viewers on 12 January [2004] by showing a decades-old film clip of a popular female Afghan singer. The broadcast marked the first time since the mujahedin [Afghan religious warriors] took control of Kabul in 1992 that a female singer was displayed on official Afghan television. Immediately, conservative Islamists cried out that this presentation was against the code of Islam.

Nevertheless, Information and Culture Minister Sayyed Makhdum Rahin said that songs by female Afghan singers would continue to be broadcast on Afghanistan Television, adding that the new constitution affords men and women equal rights, including in the arts. However, another member of Karzai's government, Deputy Chief Justice Fazl Ahmad Manawi, called the broadcast of female singers an act against the provision of the new Afghan Constitution.

Karzai, while supporting the broadcast of female singers, rather ambiguously allowed room for more debate on the matter. He stated that "Afghanistan has had women singing in the Afghan radio and television for now over 50–60 years," and people have welcomed the broadcasting of women singers on television. However, Karzai gave the Islamists room to maneuver by adding that all sides "have to work in the context of today's cultural and social environment and do whatever is suited for that."

> *"Even before [Afghan president] Hamid Karzai signed the new constitution into law, [there was] controversy . . . between the conservative Islamists and the [moderates]."*

Commenting on the issue of the broadcasting of female singers, a Herat-based [in western Afghanistan] publication wrote that "as the guardian of Islamic values and the constitution," the Afghan leader "should use his power to prevent any action that contravenes Islamic laws and values and, as a consequence, fulfill his responsibility for Islam, religion, and society."

Costly Concessions

The problem of Article 3 of the constitution stems from the fact that those who pushed for a presidential system were forced to concede something to the political camp led by the former mujahedin leaders, who initially favored a parliamentary system. The role of Islam in the Afghan Constitution, which many observers predicted would cause much controversy, did not cause significant open debate at the Loya Jirga. This could partly be due to the fact that as a compromise for accepting a strong presidential system, the mujahedin leaders won concessions on various matters related to the role of Islam in the new constitution. This trade-off resulted in the added provision that no law in Afghanistan could be "contrary to the beliefs and provisions" of Islam. This very significant clause basically gives the official and nonofficial religious leaders in Afghanistan sway over every action that they might deem contrary to their beliefs, which by extension and within the Afghan cultural context, could be regarded as "beliefs" of Islam. The use of preemptive symbolic language to secure a relatively smooth approval of the new Afghan Constitution may entail high costs in the future.

Afghanistan Is Becoming a Narco-Mafia State

by April Witt

About the author: *April Witt, who specializes in south and central Asian affairs, is a staff writer at the* Washington Post, *a daily newspaper published in Washington, D.C.*

[In] Jata [in the northeast of] Afghanistan the village mullah [religious leader] and his superior are smeared with fresh opium sap. It is harvest time, and the holy men are laboring in their poppy field, breaking the laws of Islam and Afghanistan to ease their poverty.

As the day wanes, they wait, fingers aching, for the ubiquitous young men who cross the countryside on shiny new motorbikes, buying up the deadly harvest reaped by local farmers.

"Of course it bothers me," said Mohammad Sarwar, 49, the mawlawi, or authority on Islamic teachings, at the mosque in this tiny northeastern village. "But we have to cultivate it in the current situation where we've had to borrow money, sell household items and don't have enough to eat. This is an emergency."

The drug trade in Afghanistan is growing more pervasive, powerful and organized, its corrupting reach extending to all aspects of society, according to dozens of interviews with international and Afghan anti-narcotics workers, police, poppy farmers, government officials and their critics.

Afghanistan, the world's largest opium producer last year [2002] appears poised to produce another bumper crop. In rural areas where wheat has historically been the dominant crop, fields of brilliant red, pink and white poppies are proliferating. Many poor farmers, who complain that the Afghan government and other countries have failed to ease their economic woes through legal means, say that they are growing illegal opium poppies for the first time.

At the same time, drug laboratories where raw opium is processed into morphine or heroin—once rare in Afghanistan—are sprouting at an unprecedented rate, police and anti-narcotics workers say. Many authorities appear less inclined to combat new drug syndicates than to share in their profits. The crude but money-making factories are largely condoned by elders, unmolested by police and guarded by militiamen and their commanders.

In the district of Daryian in Badakhshan province [in northeast Afghanistan] police chief Abdul Qadeer Raashed said in an interview that he had shut down and destroyed all drug laboratories in villages under his control more than one month ago, after local competitors accused him of running labs and smuggling drugs.

But a *Washington Post* reporter who insisted on touring the supposedly defunct laboratories with Qadeer on short notice found the four fire pits of one lab, at a home in the village of Langar [a border town in northeast Afghanistan], still hot to the touch, with firewood smoldering outside.

Hidden in a storeroom and outbuildings—along with the half-eaten lunches of people who had clearly been working there a short time before—were the supplies and equipment needed to produce morphine and heroin. Among them: dozens of empty oil barrels and still-damp vats for mixing and boiling, sacks of lime, more than 50 bags of chemicals such as ammonium chloride and filters for refining.

In the main house was a roster listing workers' names and duties, instructions for using a satellite telephone, and—hidden under a mound of carpets and cushions—bags of a brown powder that appeared to be heroin. While the reporter searched the property, Qadeer stood by, looking miserable.

"Come back in 48 hours," Qadeer said, "and I promise you, this will all be gone."

A Narco-Mafia State in the Making

As Afghanistan tries to put two decades of chaos and combat behind it and move toward rebuilding itself into a stable country, the growing drug trade and the corruption it is spawning threaten to make moot the ongoing debates over such basic issues as law and governance. Left unchecked, worried critics say, this will turn Afghanistan into a narco-mafia state.

Finance Minister Ashraf Ghani called the drug trade "a threat to democracy" as Afghanistan tries to prepare for elections next year [2004]. "Elections are expensive propositions," he said in an interview last week [July 2003] in the capital, Kabul. "The liquid funds from drugs, in the absence of solid institutions, could corrupt voting practices and turn them into a nightmare instead of a realization of the public will."

> *"The drug trade in Afghanistan is growing more pervasive, powerful and organized, its corrupting reach extending to all aspects of society."*

Analysts and observers say that many well-placed politicians, police officers and military officials already are profiting from the drug trade. A high-ranking anti-narcotics official recalled discussing the problem with a U.S. general, who "asked me if I could give him a list of these officials who were involved. I told him it would be easier if I listed officials who weren't involved. That would be a shorter list."

The History of Opium Production

While the opium poppy has been cultivated in Afghanistan since the 18th century, the drug trade did not flourish here until recent decades, according to a U.N. [United Nations] study published this year.

After the 1979 Soviet invasion sparked a decade-long guerrilla war fought by U.S.-backed Islamic resistance forces, the Afghan government lost control of the rugged hinterlands and never fully regained it. Through the Soviet war and the years of conflict that followed, almost every faction funded itself at least partly through the drug trade.

The seemingly endless fighting also destroyed Afghanistan's agricultural infrastructure—in particular the irrigation canals essential for nurturing crops and the roads needed to get them to market. Poor farmers increasingly turned to opium to support their families. The opium poppy requires less water than wheat, and the valuable sap it produces could be sold quickly to dealers in the fields or kept indefinitely on a farmhouse shelf and used as barter whenever a family needed something from the local bazaar.

> *"Efforts last year to stop cultivation by paying farmers to eradicate their poppy fields only encouraged more to grow it this year in the hope that they would be paid again."*

In 1999, Afghanistan produced its largest opium crop to date: 5,060 tons, from about 224,000 acres of land, according to the U.N. Office on Drugs and Crime. The following year, the Taliban, the radical Islamic movement that ruled most of the country, banned cultivation of the opium poppy, but not its trade. As a result, the price of opium soared and the Taliban reportedly profited hugely from selling stockpiles of the narcotic. Poppy cultivation plummeted, except in Badakhshan province and other areas not under Taliban control.

After the U.S.-led military campaign in late 2001 toppled the Taliban, the new president, Hamid Karzai, banned every aspect of the drug trade. Governors in some traditional poppy-growing provinces cooperated with aggressive eradication programs, but the poppy has spread rapidly in many areas where it traditionally had not been grown.

As they do every year, U.N. surveyors are trying to quantify this year's poppy harvest using satellite photography and field inspections. Their findings will be announced in September, but some surveyors say anecdotal evidence already points to an extraordinary year.

In one corner of the Borek district in Badakhshan, for example, Said Amir, a

U.N. surveyor, said that "last year I could not find one poppy there. This year it's on about 40 percent of the land."

There is broad agreement among anti-drug workers, aid agencies and poppy farmers that efforts last year to stop cultivation by paying farmers to eradicate their poppy fields only encouraged more to grow it this year in the hope that they would be paid again. And because aid groups have made food more plentiful, some farmers are feeding their families donated wheat, leaving their fields free for planting poppy.

In the northern province of Faryab, for example, World Food Program workers said they noticed the greatest poppy cultivation in areas where they distributed wheat most heavily. In the remote Garziwan district, accessible only by donkey or horse, villagers who used to travel to pick up donated wheat told aid workers that they could not be bothered. Newly flushed with opium profits, they wanted the wheat only if aid workers delivered it to them.

The Growing Power of Drug Dealers

In Badakhshan province, known for the tenacity of its opposition to the Taliban and the beauty of its mountainous terrain, the drug trade is exerting a gravitational pull on the local economy and power structure.

The increase of poppy fields and drug labs has driven the price of a day's labor from about $3 to $10—beyond the reach of farmers tending low-priced legal crops, but affordable for poppy growers.

The rising labor costs have also stalled road and bridge projects and other reconstruction efforts that are desperately needed in the province, which is poor even by Afghan standards, said Mohammad Hakim, 30, political officer for the Badakhshan office of the U.N. mission in Afghanistan.

"Almost all the U.N. projects have stopped because there is no labor," he said. "People are working with the poppy. Roof construction, school projects—all stopped. Everybody is affected."

Last year, Hakim said, several militia commanders scattered throughout the province tried to halt the spread of poppy cultivation and drug-processing labs. "This year, there was only one," he said. "Next year, maybe none. In some districts, the commander is the owner of the factory. The people who are getting involved are getting powerful."

Cmdr. Fazel Ahmad Nazari, head of criminal investigations for the Badakhshan police, said: "Day by day, it's growing more organized. If it keeps going like this we won't be able to combat it, ever."

The Drug Problem Is Out of Control

As the drug trade spreads, law enforcement efforts to combat it remain rudimentary.

The fledgling national government's new Counter-Narcotics Department is still struggling to establish itself. Kabul-based anti-narcotics police units are largely in the planning and training stages. No one is seriously investigating official drug corruption. "We don't have the capacity yet," said Mirwais Yasini, director general of the Counter-Narcotics Department.

> *"Police across the country . . . do not have the might to confront well-armed drug smugglers."*

In the eastern province of Logar, convoys of trucks loaded with drugs and guarded by men armed with semiautomatic weapons and rocket-propelled grenade launchers travel toward Pakistani border at least two or three times a week. The police chief says that his men don't have the firepower to stop them and that some well-armed militiamen are in league with the smugglers.

"It's out of our control," said Maj. Gen. Noor Mohammad Pakteen, who has been a law enforcement officer for 36 of his 59 years. "The drug mafia is getting worse daily. When nobody will help us, we can't do anything. . . . I'm so frustrated, actually, I'm ready to leave my job."

Police across the country not only do not have the might to confront well-armed drug smugglers, they also lack such basics as cars, telephones and radios.

In mountainous Badakhshan, the police have just one vehicle, a pickup truck. When police at headquarters in the provincial capital, Faizabad, receive a tip about a smuggling operation in a far-flung district, Nazari often has to send an officer on foot. A round trip can take a month and leave an officer in trouble with no way to call for help.

"These mafia who are very active in Afghanistan have everything," Nazari said. "They have motorbikes, pistols, mobile phones and tight communication. The police who are trying to combat those smugglers have nothing."

Police in Badakhshan are supposed to receive a monthly salary of up to 1,500 afghanis—about $30. But the national government had failed to pay them for months at a time.

A demoralized police officer is ripe for bribes. "For $100, he'll be hired," Nazari said. "The drug smugglers will give him some money and tell that even though he knows about a laboratory he should say that he doesn't. It's happened lots of times."

Growing Opium to Survive

The elder of Boymalasi village—a doctor—last year criticized the spread of poppy fields throughout the Argo district of Badakhshan. This year he's growing poppy.

"I feel 100 percent terrible about it," said Hasamudin, 44, looking down at his feet. "There is no rule in Afghanistan. If there was rule, the people could not do this. They would have to obey the orders of the government. There is no government in Afghanistan, just the name of government. Who will come and ask us about our crime?"

Ghulam Mohammad, 60, expressed no such misgivings. He has lived most of his life in a one-room house in Argo [a district in northeast Afghanistan] farming wheat on a small plot to support his family of 10. "We never had a good life," he said.

This season he and his son-in-law Safar planted poppy. Mohammad borrowed against anticipated profits of $1,800—30 times more than he ever earned selling wheat, he said—to add three rooms to his house.

Nobody, not even the local mullahs [Islamic scholars], is telling the wizened farmer and his neighbors that what they are doing is wrong. In fact, they laugh at the notion.

"In my village, the mullah himself has cultivated it," said Safar, 45.

"All the mullahs are cultivating it," Mohammad said.

Along the banks of the nearby Kokcha River, Mullah Abdul Rashid of the Jata mosque is indeed laboring in his poppy field. Working with his business partner—Sarwar, the mosque's mawlawi—the mullah deftly slices one ovoid poppy pod after another to release opium sap. All 80 families in their village are growing poppy this year, the clerics said.

"Of course we believe that growing this poppy will have a very bad moral effect on the people of Badakhshan," said the mullah, 36. "In the future, we hope it will be eradicated. Now, it's everywhere because the people need it to survive.

"I won't allow anyone to eradicate this field," the mullah said. "In the future, if my situation got better, I'll destroy it myself."

Chapter 2

Has the Human Rights Situation in Afghanistan Improved Since the Fall of the Taliban?

Chapter Preface

The September 11, 2001, terrorist attacks on the United States drew world attention to Afghanistan. The terrorists responsible for the attacks were part of the terrorist group al Qaeda, which was being harbored by the Taliban regime in Afghanistan. People in Western countries were shocked and outraged by the human rights abuses suffered by the Afghan people, especially the women. Under the Islamic fundamentalist Taliban regime, Afghan women were forbidden to go to school or to work outside the home. Some women were beaten for laughing out loud, flogged for having their hair or feet show from under their burkas (long black robes), or punished for wearing nail polish by having their finger nails ripped out. "Civilized people are speaking out in horror. . . . Our hearts break for the women . . . of Afghanistan," said First Lady Laura Bush in a presidential radio address on November 17, 2001.

In early 2002, after U.S.-led forces ousted the Taliban, Laura Bush led an international effort to support the new Afghan government's initiatives to improve women's lives. With foreign support, the government opened schools for girls and created the Ministry of Women's Affairs. They passed laws allowing women to go to work and to appear in public without their burkas. Many commentators, including Laura Bush, applauded these developments as signs of the liberation of Afghan women from the dark days of fundamentalism.

By mid 2003, however, commentators revised their conclusions when the U.S.-based nonprofit agency Human Rights Watch released a survey on the human rights situation in Afghanistan. According to the survey, Afghan women, particularly those who lived outside the main cities, were still harassed, kidnapped, and raped by fundamentalist warlords. As 2003 progressed, the women's situation worsened when the Taliban, having regrouped in Pakistan, returned to Afghanistan. Taliban militia burned down girls' schools and went so far, according to Islamic press reports, as to poison young schoolgirls to deter female students from attending school.

In response to the escalating violence, Afghan women and girls demonstrated their determination to stand their ground. Throughout Afghanistan, schoolgirls courageously defied the Taliban's threats and pursued their education. In one press report in early September 2003, twelve schoolgirls in Mughal Khel village, forty miles south of Kabul, were photographed taking lessons sitting among the ashes of their former tent-classroom, which the Taliban had burned to the ground the previous night. "This . . . [illustrates] very strongly . . . the determination of the young students who simply refused to stay at home, a day after their school was burned to ashes," said Afghan president Hamid Karzai.

Further evidence of the determination of Afghan women to claim their rights as equal human beings in Afghan society came in late September 2003. Forty-five women, representing every region in Afghanistan, withstood fundamentalists' threats and presented the Afghan Women's Bill of Rights to Karzai. In the document the women demanded government protection from abuse and equal rights under the law. The first of its type in the Muslim world, the Afghan Women's Bill of Rights has become a source of inspiration to oppressed women worldwide and suggests that, after their first taste of the rights and freedoms accorded most women in the modern world, it is unlikely the women of Afghanistan will be silenced. The authors in the following chapter explore this and other issues related to the status of human rights in Afghanistan.

Afghanistan's Independent Human Rights Commission Is Protecting Human Rights

by Sima Samar

About the author: *Sima Samar is the chairperson of the Afghan Independent Human Rights Commission (AIHRC). AIHRC was established by a presidential decree on June 6, 2002, in accordance with the Bonn Agreement signed in Germany between representatives of international community and the transitional Islamic government of Afghanistan. AIHRC consists of eleven commissioners who are mandated to promote and protect human rights in Afghanistan. Prior to chairing the AIHRC, Samar was the first deputy chair and the minister of Women's Affairs of Afghanistan's transitional government.*

The Afghan Independent Human Rights Commission was established in 2002 according to the Bonn Agreement[1] and a presidential decree announced on 6th of June. The initial term of service was two years, but fortunately the Commission is included as a permanent institution in Afghanistan's new Constitution which was adopted in January this year [2004]. This gives our people and our colleagues in the Commission the opportunity to continue the struggle to promote and protect human rights in Afghanistan.

We started our activities just five days after the establishment of the Commission without budget or any other means for work. We were only 11 commissioners. Today we have our main office in the capital, and seven regional offices

---

1. The Bonn Agreement was signed on December 5, 2001, between representatives of the international community and Afghanistan's interim administration. Following the defeat of the Islamic fundamentalist Taliban regime, the agreement set up an interim government and administration until general elections could be organized to establish a permanent government in Afghanistan.

Sima Samar, address to the 8th Annual Meeting of the Asia Pacific Forum of National Human Rights Institutions, Kathmandu, Nepal, February 16–18, 2004.

in different parts of the country. Today, the number of executive staff including support personnel is about 300 people. Our Commission is nearly gender-balanced, with five women and six men.

We have developed our 5-year strategic plan. The Commission has set up its working sections in the main office as well as in the regional offices. These sections are Human Rights Education, Women's Rights Promotion, Child Rights Promotion, Monitoring and Investigation of Human Rights Violations, and Transitional Justice.

> *"After the grave violations of human rights in Afghanistan—where using the word of human right was counted as crime—this is the first Human Rights Commission in our history."*

After the grave violations of human rights in Afghanistan—where using the word of human right was counted as crime—this is the first Human Rights Commission in our history. Working in this field in a country like Afghanistan where the gun still rules is not an easy task. To be able to promote and protect the human rights, we have held more then 250 workshops and trainings to build the capacity of our staff and to train others in the related governmental, NGO's [nongovernmental organizations] and civil society about human rights. We have run these programs in Kabul and in our regional offices.

As a result of our lobbying, Afghanistan Government ratified CEDAW [Convention of the Elimination of All Forms of Discrimination Against Women], ICC [International Criminal Court], and Optional Protocol II of CRC[2] last year [2003]. Our Commission also successfully campaigned among the delegates of the [Constitutional] Grand Assembly [of people's representatives who met to negotiate the new constitution] in January 2004 for inclusion in the new constitution of the bill of rights based on the international standards.

Activities to Promote a Just and Non-Violent World

Our Commission so far has registered over 2000 complaints of human rights violations, which we have received from different parts of the country. Of greatest concern, the violations include cases of land dispute, forced marriage, child kidnapping and trafficking, domestic and sexual violence, torture, arbitrary detention, and violation of the rights of detainees and prisoners.

Our staff regularly monitors the detention centers, prisons, and child rehabilitation centers as well as the other cases of violation and abuses of human rights. We report back to the President and other relevant organizations in efforts to stop the violations and to seek justice and remedies. Some of the reports are published widely in our monthly magazine.

While our Commission is in the preliminary stage of developing its institu-

---

2. additional covenants to the UN Convention on the Rights of the Child, which prohibits the recruitment of children under 18 for military purposes

tional capacity, we hope that we can become members of [the Asia Pacific Forum of National Human Rights Institutions], which plays a vital role in sharing experiences among the national human rights institutions in the region, strengthening our efforts, and supporting each other.

At the end I would like to thank the International community and donors [who] make our work possible in Afghanistan. . . .

I hope for peace, equality, justice, and a non-violent world.

Afghanistan Has Made Progress in Improving the Lives of Its Women and Children

by Edward Carwardine

About the author: *Edward Carwardine is the communication officer for the United Nations Children's Fund (UNICEF) in Afghanistan. UNICEF is the major UN agency dedicated to promoting the health, welfare, and education of women and children in the developing world.*

Three years since the fall of the Taliban regime in Afghanistan, the United Nations Children's Fund this week highlights some of the progress that has been made for the country's women and children since the start of the reconstruction process.

Emphasising the prominent role of the Transitional Government, national NGOs [nongovernmental organizations] and the Afghan people, UNICEF has applauded its partners for the unparalleled progress seen in areas such as health, nutrition, water and sanitation, education and the protection of children's rights.

UNICEF Acting Representative in Afghanistan, Dr. Waheed Hassan, said today "In the last three years a number of important steps have been made in advancing the welfare of Afghanistan's children and women. In the area of health, we have seen 16 million children immunized against measles, some 6 million children immunized against polio each year, and more than 3 million women have received life-saving tetanus vaccinations. The status of mothers' health has improved, with the opening of new centres of excellence in maternal health in Kabul, Herat and Jalalabad, the refurbishment of provincial obstetric care facilities in every province, and with the training of obstetricians and midwives across the country. Five salt iodation plants have opened, which will greatly reduce the prevalence of mental and physical stunting and goitre, while 5 million children have benefited from Vitamin A supplementation in both 2002 and 2003."

In the area of education, Hassan pointed to huge increases in the number of children enrolled in Afghanistan's schools. "Demand for learning has exceeded all expectation; more than 4 million children are now attending classes in every community in the country—that's more than ever before in Afghanistan's history. 1.2 million of those students—one-third—are girls, and in just two years we saw the boy:girl ratio in education return to pre-Taliban levels. That means that a seven year education deficit was wiped out in just 24 months. More women teachers are returning to the classrooms, and we have seen significant improvements in the quality of education, with 50,000 teachers being trained this year alone in new methodologies and key progress made in the area of curriculum development. By next year, we expect to see a fully updated, student-friendly curriculum in place at primary level."

Promoting Child Protection and National Capacity

Education has also provided opportunities to promote health and child protection measures; over the last three years, some 2 million school children have participated in hygiene promotion sessions integrated into the national curriculum, while water and sanitation facilities have been constructed in more than 500 schools. 25,000 teachers have been trained in mine risk education, and we have seen a related reduction in the number of children being killed or injured by landmines and unexploded ordnance every month.

> *"UNICEF has applauded its partners for the unparalleled progress seen in . . . health, nutrition, water and sanitation, education and . . . children's rights."*

The past three years have also seen a number of new developments. In 2003, the first ever birth registration programme was launched in Afghanistan; since then 1.2 million children under the age of five have been registered. The campaign is unique in that it utilises the services of polio vaccinators, combining the birth registration effort with Afghanistan's National Polio Immunization Days held throughout the year.

In support of the national disarmament process, UNICEF has supported a special programme to assist war-affected young people, including former child soldiers, to return to mainstream life. 4,000 children are benefiting from vocational training and literacy classes, in a programme that is run and managed by local communities themselves, while more than 3,000 former child soldiers have been demobilised.

Hassan also pointed to the important progress made in the area of national capacity within the Transitional Government. "UNICEF has always seen its role in Afghanistan as being a key partner of Government," he explained. "The support we offer Government, at central, provincial and district level, is designed to empower the people of Afghanistan to design and manage their own services and programmes for children and women. In every sector, we have been proud to provide practical, tangible assistance in areas such as training, expert advice on policy development, as well as physical improvements to Ministry offices and health and education infrastructure—including a new education logistics centre and Afghanistan's first national cold store for vaccines."

Commenting on the challenges still ahead, the UNICEF Acting Representative called for continued international assistance to Afghanistan. "Afghanistan is at a crucial stage of the reconstruction process," he said. "The progress made so far for children and women has reached out to every household. The programmes for women and children are an outstanding example of how reconstruction helps to rebuild not just local communities but a nation as a whole. The foundations are certainly in place but we have to continue building. We need to build a health system that will stop one child in six dying before its fifth birthday. We need to ensure that every girl attends school, and that every student receives a quality education. We need to ensure that those young people who were denied the right to learning because of a generation of conflict are able to develop new skills that will make them productive members of society. We need to give back the right to a safe motherhood to every woman in Afghanistan, and deliver community-based maternal health services that will prevent one woman dying every 20 minutes as a result of complications in childbirth and pregnancy."

Hassan reassured the people of Afghanistan of UNICEF's long-term commitment to the reconstruction process. "UNICEF never left Afghanistan over the last five decades. Even in the darkest hours, our Afghan staff continued to deliver vital services for children and women. That dedication to the rights of Afghanistan's mothers and children continues, and is strengthened by the progress we have seen in such a short time. But with other global issues now attracting international interest, it is crucial that Afghanistan does not slip from the donors' radar screen. If it does, then the world will have failed the very women and children that it promised never to forget just three years ago."

Afghan Women's Lives Have Improved

by Sally Armstrong

About the author: *Sally Armstrong is a Canadian journalist and the special representative to Afghanistan for the United Nations Children's Fund (UNICEF). She is also the author of* Veiled Threat: The Hidden Power of the Women of Afghanistan, *in which she interviews Afghan women before and after the fall of the Taliban.*

In the winter of 2001, I decided to travel to Kandahar [in southeast Afghanistan], the spiritual capital of the Taliban [Islamic fundamentalist former rulers of Afghanistan], to see conditions for myself. Gaining entrance to this place as a woman, a journalist and a foreigner—all red flags to the ruling Taliban—required patience and downright chicanery. I needed to invent a cover. I had learned several months earlier that Canada was funding a non-government organization called Guardians, which was doing excellent work at the Institute for Orthopedics in Kandahar. I thought there might be a match between its purposes and mine: they wanted publicity for the Institute and I wanted to report firsthand on how women were faring under the Taliban. I left Toronto armed with a visa for Pakistan, knowing I'd then have to negotiate a visa for Afghanistan. There a Taliban functionary told me the photo in my passport was not acceptable since "the woman is smiling and the yellow hair is showing." Then he announced that because I am a woman, I could only travel if accompanied by a man.

The regional director of Guardians in Afghanistan, Zalmai Mojadidi, agreed to fill the role of requisite male. At the border passport office, Mojadidi had some advice. "No say hello with your hand. Smile is okay but not so much. And no your laughing, please." We'd already had a discussion about wardrobe, and he explained that only an Afghan woman had the right to wear a burka. I wondered how it could be considered a "right" to wear a head-to-ankle body bag with a little piece of mesh in front of the eyes. We agreed that I would wear my ankle-length heavy gray winter coat, with a huge black chador wrapped around my hips, shoulders and head, which made it difficult to see, hear and walk, not to mention climb out of a truck without showing my legs.

In Kandahar the uneasy rhythms of life for Afghan women were evident everywhere, including the Institute for Orthopedics—with its Canadian flag pasted to the front wall standing out like a monument. It was modern by central Asian standards, and it was treating about 1,000 dismembered and disabled Afghan citizens a month, most maimed by some of the estimated 10 million land mines scattered throughout the country. The Canadian government had stipulated their funds were dependent on women being treated and employed as well as men. Indeed, in the basement of this two-storey structure, eight women were treating disabled women who were hidden from the men upstairs.

Oppression of Women Under the Taliban

It was there that I met secretly with a group of women to talk about their lives under the Taliban. They shed the burkas—which make them look like clones of one another—and the contrast was shocking. Under those alienating veils were pretty, vibrant, engaging women. They were teachers before the Taliban closed the schools in Kandahar. Now they were sitting behind windows painted over so no one could see them. They weren't allowed to send their own daughters to school.

As women do, they made the visit unforgettable, with stories about their families, kibitzing about the job, and offers of cups of the traditional green tea and delicious, hot naan bread. I noticed they wore shoes with wedges and asked why they are all the same. At first they responded as if by rote and said, "High-heeled shoes are un-Islamic." I gestured to the painted windows and asked them how they put up with this nonsense. One woman blurted out, "It's unbearable." The others quickly hushed her. Then they looked at each other and the floodgates opened. "Look at this place, it's like a jail. Women are nothing in Afghanistan today. And our shoes, they're awful. We have to wear them because the Taliban don't like the tap-tap-tap of women's high-heeled shoes. We hate having to do this." They told me of a friend who went to jail for 30 days because she invited a foreigner to a family wedding, and another who was jailed for 15 days because she spoke to a man on the street. Every day was a struggle to buy enough food to feed their children. They were trying to keep their kids in the clandestine schools, but the classes were stopped so often that

> *"I met secretly with a group of women to talk about their lives under the Taliban."*

their education had become hit and miss, mostly miss.

During the time I spent listening to the extraordinary events of their lives, the women and I laughed and cried together. We made friends with each other. When I left, they tucked pieces of bread and sweet cakes into my pockets for the long journey out of their country. I knew I would never forget the sweet-faced Sharifa Reza Mohseny and the good-humoured, witty Frozan Mahram and her comical friend Sima Shahnawaz and the other women who worked with them. Nor would I forget their little children who were paying such a terrible price for the wreckage the merciless regime had inflicted on the country. It was truly humbling to receive from women who need so much to be given to them. They had the grace to worry about the comfort of someone else's voyage out of a country that had become their prison.

> *"They implored me to take their story to the world outside, to ask the women in the world to help them."*

In the kind of Alice Through The Looking Glass contradiction that seems to be everywhere in Afghanistan, I learned that the Institute also provided prosthetics for those who had lost limbs in the grisly amputations mandated by the Taliban's interpretation of Sharia [Islamic] law. For stealing, the thief lost a hand, for stealing again, a foot. Therapist Zareen Khan was quick to point out, "The thief receives an injection of anaesthetic before the removal of the limb and so it is painless." Not so for women who were sentenced to death by stoning for alleged illicit relations. There was no numbing their pain. In fact, the Taliban's Sharia stated that the stones thrown not be so big as to kill them quickly.

When I bid farewell to the women I met during that voyage, their canny analysis and witty descriptions about their lives under the Taliban gave way to darker realities. With trepidation and in barely audible whispers, they implored me to take their story to the world outside, to ask the women in the world to help them. They said, "Get our schools open, get us back to work, or get us out of here."

The Liberation of Women After the Defeat of the Taliban

On Feb. 8 [2002], I returned to the country in the wake of the U.S. bombing campaign that overthrew the Taliban. I wanted to find out what was happening to women in Kabul and to try to find Sharifa and Frozan and the other women I'd met in Kandahar just one year earlier. The street scene was the first sign of change. Crowds of men and woman walked on the street. While the vast majority of women still wore burkas, change was clearly happening from the bottom up. Forced to wear wedge-heeled shoes during the Taliban era, and forbidden to wear white socks or any other form of stocking that might attract attention, the women of Kabul were making a statement, feet-first. Platform shoes, high heels, patent-leather pumps were everywhere. And hosiery was patterned, coloured and very much on display. Even the burkas at a jaunty angle, displaying dresses. Hands, formerly hidden, were very much in evidence while women walked together, talking, gesturing, and even returning the thumbs-up sign to me when we passed on the street. There was a palpable air of excitement in the city—and music, which had also been forbidden, was playing at every little kiosk. Women were working again and not wearing burkas in the offices. Girls' schools had re-opened, and the students were trying to catch up on what they had missed. And the girls were writing entrance exams to get back to university.

When I arrived in Kandahar, the shrieks and laughter of children at play filled the air, a sound I had never heard during the Taliban occupation, when children were forbidden to play, even with their own toys. We drove to the Institute of Orthopedics and, to my surprise, the first person to greet me was Zalmai Mojadidi, my former fixer. "Your girls are waiting for you," he said jubilantly. And suddenly there they were—Sharifa, Frozan, Sima, Torpeky, Zarghona and Rozia. The reunion was wonderful, exhilarating, and very emotional. Everyone talked at once, telling me where they'd been during the American bombing, how they felt when the Taliban were defeated. And each one in turn shared her hopes for tomorrow. "Now we have freedom," said Frozan Mahram. "Every girl can go to school. We can watch TV, walk in the street. If a woman wants to wear a burka or not, she can. We can choose our own husbands and they don't have to have beards."

Sima Shanawaz, who had been married just a month before we met in January, 2001, put her new baby boy, Tariq, into my arms and said, "See what I did." The paint had been scrubbed off the windows in their therapy department, and their wedge shoes replaced with fashionable pumps. Sharifa Reza Mohseny said her six children could now have an education. Her daughter Sima, 15, who hadn't been to school in five years, told me she wanted to be a doctor and take care of the sick people in Kandahar.

Life was looking very different from the ordeal they were living through when last we met. "The bazaar is full of video cassettes and music," said Sima.

> *"Women were working again and not wearing burkas in the offices. Girls' schools had re-opened, and the students were trying to catch up on what they had missed."*

"People are singing and dancing. There are marriage ceremonies. We watch American films on television." The rapid-fire accounts of their lives then were told as though to annul the long years they lived in what seemed to be a prison. They told me they wanted to travel, to see foreign countries, to have peace and freedom. They wanted education, a modern lifestyle, streets and hospitals that functioned. They used to be afraid of everything, even the staff at this centre, even each other at times.

We had tea and talked about families and promised to stay in touch. They posed for a photo with me and said, "This time you can use our family names and our faces. We're safe now. We're not afraid anymore."

The Afghan Government Has Assisted the Safe Return and Reintegration of Afghan Refugees

by the Consultative Group on Refugees and Internally Displaced Persons in Afghanistan

About the author: *The Consultative Group on Refugees and Internally Displaced Persons (IDPs) in Afghanistan is a consortium of United Nations, government, and nongovernment agencies that was established by the Afghan Ministry of Refugees and Repatriation to coordinate and assist with the resettlement of refugees to Afghanistan.*

The aim of the Transitional Islamic State of Afghanistan's *National Return, Displacement and Reintegration Strategy* is to support the voluntary return, in safety and dignity, and the initial reintegration of Afghan refugees and Internally Displaced Persons (IDPs) in their chosen communities and to provide protection, and humanitarian assistance and solutions to residual IDPs.

The Ministry of Refugees and repatriation (MoRR), in close cooperation with UNHCR [United Nations High Commissioner on Refugees], UN agencies, and NGOs [nongovernmental organizations] (international and local) is implementing *the refugee and IDP programme.* Its objective is the voluntary return and sustainable reintegration of refugees and IDPs into communities and homes of their choice. It addresses immediate return and initial reintegration challenges; medium and longer term assistance to returnees and returnee impacted areas is provided primarily through the Livelihoods and Social Protection programmes, implemented by the MRRD.

The Ministry of Refugees and Repatriation, UNHCR along with partner agencies and NGOs:

Consultative Group on Refugees and Internally Displaced Persons in Afghanistan, *Securing Afghanistan's Future: Accomplishments and the Strategic Path Forward*, January 2004.

i.   assists sustainable returns which are voluntary, safe and gradual;

ii. assists the voluntary return of and/or finding durable solutions for IDPs;

iii. supports reintegration needs through the provision of rural housing, water, sanitation and income generation, in coordination with the Ministry of Rural Rehabilitation and Development, and the Ministry of Urban Development and Housing;

iv. assists capacity building of national institutions for displacement and reintegration; and

v.   establishes operational links with rehabilitation, reconstruction and development initiatives.

The current programme's sub objectives are: (i) Returnees from Pakistan, Iran, and elsewhere, and IDPs return home voluntarily in safety and dignity. (ii) IDPs who cannot return home are provided with security, protection, and essential assistance pending durable solutions. (iii) Returnees from asylum countries and IDPs are supported with initial reintegration assistance to address key short term needs.

Government Programs

There are five sub programmes currently under implementation:

i.   Refugees and IDP—repatriation and return

ii. Assistance to the residual IDP population

iii. Initial returnee reintegration

iv. Refugees and IDPs—protection and social services

v.   Refugees and IDPs—capacity building

The total budget request for year 1382 [2002] was US$164 million.

Some of the impacts of the activities within the framework of this programme have been:

Returnees and IDPs: Up until the end of November 2003, an overall total of over 3 million persons have returned to their homes. These figures include 2,270,000 persons who have been assisted to repatriate voluntarily to Afghanistan from 17 different countries, more than 226,000 persons who have returned spontaneously and without assistance mostly from Iran, and approximately 600,000 IDPs. Returnees were provided with Mine Risk Education in camps across the country. UNHCR provided returnees with return transport grants amounting to a total of more than $30 million in 2002 and $3.5 million in 2003. In addition to pre-departure interviews, iris recognition technology was successfully activated at all voluntary registration centers for returnees from Pakistan as a measure to prevent individuals from benefiting more than once from assistance.

> *"Over 3 million persons . . . have been assisted to repatriate voluntarily to Afghanistan from 17 different countries."*

IDPs: Up to the present approximately 600,000 IDPs have returned to their places of origin in 2003 from the south and west of the country. In addition, some 200,000 IDPs have been locally integrated. Essential assistance has been provided to IDP camps in both southern and western Afghanistan to those who have not yet made the decision to return home. Re-verification exercises of the remaining IDPs in the south have been undertaken. Efforts to find durable solutions (return or local settlement) have been encouraged. Due to humanitarian concerns, relocation to more secure and accessible camps in Afghanistan or Pakistan has been exceptionally undertaken for one group stranded at the Chaman border.

Immediate Assistance: over 6,000 metric tons of wheat and 244 metric tons of non food items were distributed by WFP [World Food Program] 80,000 plastic sheets, 80,000 meters of hygienic cloth, and over 120,000 kg of soap were distributed by UNHCR. Assistance both in kind (food aid, non-food items, cash grants) to a total value of US$60 million has been given to returning refugees who collect their entitlements at one of the 12 encashment/distribution centers set up around the country. Returnees are also helped with transport grants ranging from US$ 3–30 depending on their destination.

Shelter: By the end of 2003, it is forecast that a total of approximately 90,000 shelters will have been built for returning refugees, IDPs and poor members of the host communities. Total costs to date (mainly international procurement of materials) amounts to approximately 60 million dollars.

> *"Assistance . . . (food aid, non-food items, cash grants) to a total value of US$60 million has been given to returning refugees."*

Water and sanitation: By the end of 2003, approximately 4,500 water points (shallow wells, dug wells, tube wells, pipe schemes) will have been constructed. The sector is covered by another programme in the National Budget and is coordinated by MRRD. Sanitation activities include the construction of 3,276 baths and 14,940 latrines.

Income Generation Activities: Income generation activities are implemented through programmes run by the MRRD but are targeted at returnees and IDPs and host communities. UNHCR and partners are implementing "cash for work" projects, which include, among others, wool spinning, agricultural activities, irrigation projects, kareze [underground water channels] cleaning and small road/bridge rehabilitation. There are also activities specifically geared towards women (such as tailoring, carpet-weaving, etc.) and related to the protection of returnees and IDPs.

Protection: Since 2002, an extensive protection presence has been established in all the six major regions of Afghanistan. It has mobilized close to 9,000 field missions in the last two years to monitor the conditions of returning refugees and IDPs, to intervene in cases of physical and material safety, to raise and pursue legal issues such as the restitution of land and property, and to advocate for the allocation of resources and support for vulnerable areas and groups (especially single women, children, old people). Information and Legal Aid Centers for returning Afghans have been established in major cities. Objective information about the situation in Afghanistan is distributed through print and electronic media to Afghans in the region to allow them to make informed decisions about return. UNHCR returnee monitoring teams assisted returnees throughout Afghanistan, ensuring that returns are voluntary, safe and gradual.

> *"UNHCR returnee monitoring teams assisted returnees throughout Afghanistan, ensuring that returns are voluntary, safe and gradual."*

Policy: the CG assisted the Government in preparing a National Return, Displacement and Reintegration Strategy for 1382 [2002] and an IDP strategy, which was then endorsed by the Government through the Ministry of Refugees and Repatriation and the Ministry of Rural Rehabilitation and Development. The CG convened an inter-Ministerial working group (Ministry of Refugees and Repatriation, the Ministry of Rural Rehabilitation and Development and the Ministry of Urban Development and Housing) to develop and implement a strategy for urban returns, with a particular focus on winter preparedness for vulnerable returnees in Kabul.

Institutional Arrangements and Support: The Government of Afghanistan and UNHCR have signed Tripartite Agreements with Pakistan, Iran, the United Kingdom, France, the Netherlands, and a bilateral agreement with Australia since 2002. The Ministry of Refugees and Repatriation has established and chaired the Consultative Group on Refugees and IDPs. It also chairs the Return Commission set up to facilitate and manage returns of IDPs to the northern provinces. It has received technical and financial support (staffing, equipment, budget) as has the Ministry of Rural Reconstruction and Development (MRRD) for a reintegration unit. This has been instrumental in the preparation of a National Reintegration Strategy.

Continued Human Rights Abuses Threaten Afghanistan's Progress

by Human Rights Watch

About the author: *Human Rights Watch (HRW) is the largest human rights organization in the United States. With offices in Washington, D.C., Los Angeles, San Francisco, Brussels, London, and Geneva, HRW staff research and conduct fact-finding missions into human rights abuses in more than seventy countries.*

Afghanistan's human rights situation remains tenuous. Since a U.S.-led coalition ousted the Taliban [Islamic fundamentalist former rulers] in December 2001 and helped create a transitional government under President Hamid Karzai, there have been some successes in restoring essential governance, improving basic security, and building systems to ensure the rule of law. A new constitution adopted in January 2004 includes significant protections. But human rights practices have not improved markedly or indeed at all in large parts of the country.

Life outside of Kabul is dominated by military faction leaders—Afghanistan's warlords. In most areas outside the capital, independent political movements and media have been stifled: in many areas it is impossible to form political groups or freely publish newspapers or broadcast radio without incurring the wrath of local warlord leaders. Women and girls especially are suffering from insecurity and lack of protection. In some areas, security and human rights conditions have actually gotten worse, and most warlords have become more entrenched.

Abuses by Warlords and the Taliban

Since the fall of the Taliban, Human Rights Watch has documented criminality and abuses by warlord forces all over the country: those under Atta Mohammad and Rashid Dostum in the north, Ismail Khan in the west, Hazrat Ali in the east, Gul Agha Shirzai in the south, Abdul Rasul Sayyaf near the center, and, Mohammad Qasim Fahim, the senior vice president and minister of defense, in Kabul itself and surrounding areas. Many other less powerful warlords are also implicated in ongoing abuses.

The list of documented violations is extensive. Local security and police forces, even in Kabul city, are involved in arbitrary arrests, kidnapping and extortion, and torture and extrajudicial killings of criminal suspects. Outside of Kabul, commanders and their troops are implicated in extortion, intimidation of political dissidents, rape of women and girls, rape of boys, murder, illegal detention and forced displacement, as well as specific abuses against women and children, including trafficking, sexual violence, and forced marriage. High-level commanders in Kabul, Kandahar, Herat, and other cities are also involved in property seizures and forced displacement.

> *"Human rights practices have not improved markedly or indeed at all in large parts of the country."*

Local factions are not the only problem. In the south and southeast of the country, Taliban remnants and other anti-government forces outside Afghanistan's political framework have further aggravated security conditions by attacking humanitarian workers and coalition and Afghan government forces. In 2003 and early 2004, numerous humanitarian workers in the south and southeast have been kidnapped, beaten up, shot at, and even killed. Over thirty-five schools in the south and southeast, mostly for girls, have been rocketed or burned since August 2002.

As a result of attacks, international agencies have suspended many of their operations in the affected areas. As a result, development and humanitarian work has suffered.

Women and girls bear some of the worst effects of Afghanistan's insecurity. Conditions are generally are better than under the Taliban, but women and girls continue to face severe governmental and social discrimination. Those who organize protests or criticize local rulers face threats and violence. Soldiers and police routinely harass women and girls, even in Kabul city. Many women and girls are afraid to remove the burqa [head and body covering]. Because soldiers are targeting women and girls, many are staying indoors, especially in rural areas, making it impossible for them to attend school, go to work, or actively participate in the country's reconstruction. The majority of school-age girls in Afghanistan are still not enrolled in school.

The Political Process Has Entrenched Local Factions

Afghanistan's current political arrangements were set up under the December 2001 Bonn Agreement, a power-sharing agreement signed by representatives of various Afghan factions and a handful of other political figures invited by the

United States and United Nations. The Bonn Agreement, among other things, set up a six-month interim authority for Afghanistan and mandated a conference (the June 2002 Emergency Loya Jirga [people's assembly]) to choose a second "transitional administration" to serve though 2004, as well as a constitutional convention (the December 2003 Constitutional Loya Jirga) to choose a new charter for the country. Democratic elections for offices created under the constitution were to be held two years later, that is, in mid-2004.

The Bonn Agreement specified that separate military groups and factions were to come under the authority of the interim authority headed by President Karzai. The agreement also called on factions signing the Bonn Agreement to withdraw from Kabul city and other areas in which international forces might be deployed.

But the Bonn Process is not on track. On the surface, many of the Bonn Agreement's provisions have been honored, but in fact many of its aspirations have not been met. Overall, the political process for both the Emergency Loya Jirga and the Constitutional Loya Jirga did not increase legitimate political representation but instead entrenched existing factions.

Afghan factional forces have not unified; in some areas in the north there are regular clashes between rival groups sometimes resulting in civilian casualties. Military factions occupying Kabul have not withdrawn from the city, and efforts in January 2004 to have factions withdraw heavy weapons from the city have met with only partial success.

Limitations of the New Constitution

Despite the democratic shortcomings of the Constitutional Loya Jirga, the new Afghan constitution it approved in January 2004 included significant provisions, notably on women's rights. The constitution guarantees women a substantial number of seats in Afghanistan's bicameral National Assembly. Approximately 25 percent of seats in the Wolesi Jirga (House of the People) are reserved for women; the president is obligated to appoint additional women in the Meshrano Jirga (House of Elders). Another provision of the constitution specifically guarantees equality between men and women under law.

The document contains several provisions enunciating basic political, civil, economic, and social rights, but little strong language empowering institutions to uphold them. The Afghan Independent Human Rights Commission [AIHRC] is given a mandate, but

> *"As a result of attacks [on aid workers], international agencies have suspended many of their operations."*

lacks many of the powers necessary for it to credibly protect basic rights.

The constitution fails to adequately address the role of Islamic law and its relationship to human rights protections. Human Rights Watch is concerned that extremist factions could use appointments to the new judiciary to implement laws that violate human rights standards.

The issue of accountability for past atrocities is also not addressed in the document. Despite Afghanistan's recent history, the charter does not directly address issues of past war crimes and serious human rights abuses. The AIHRC may be able to delve further into this area, but it lacks any specific constitutional mandate to do so.

Failures of the International Community

The government of Hamid Karzai has been unable to adequately address Afghanistan's security and human rights problems, and in many cases has preferred to negotiate and cooperate with leaders implicated in abuses, as have U.S. government officials in the country, who continue to be influential actors in Afghanistan's political processes.

The international community generally has not done enough to address Afghanistan's security situation. The U.N.-mandated International Security Assistance Force (ISAF), a small body of security troops predominately comprised of Canadian and German troops, is still mostly limited to Kabul city. NATO [North Atlantic Treaty Organization], which commands the force, has stated that it wants to expand its geographic scope, but contributing nations have not promised enough additional troops.

The United States has been expanding small Provincial Reconstruction Teams (PRTs) of 50–100 troops to several areas, but they have had only limited success in improving human rights protections and security. The small size of the teams and their often close working relationship with local Afghan militias—the very forces who are creating abusive and insecure environments in the first place—have stymied further progress.

The United States, the most important and involved international actor in the country, has not taken the steps necessary to lead other nations in providing security, troops, funding, and political leadership to secure Afghanistan's future. But NATO member states and other potential troop contributors are also to blame for not providing more troops to ISAF and adequate overall funding for international efforts in Afghanistan.

The general failure of U.N. member states to provide an underlying security framework for reconstruction in Afghanistan has made it impossible for UNAMA [United Nations Assistance Mission in Afghanistan] to carry out many parts of its mandate.

But the leadership of UNAMA is also to blame for consciously limiting its criticisms of Afghan warlords and its efforts to monitor human rights and security. As a result of these decisions, no detailed and comprehensive human rights reporting is being conducted by the international community in Afghanistan, except by non-governmental groups like Human Rights Watch. To make matters worse, in its resolution on Afghanistan in 2003 the U.N. Commission on Human Rights failed to insist on improved rights monitoring and protection efforts.

The Afghan People Are Still Terrorized and Exploited

by Noor Beasharat

About the author: Noor Beasharat is an Afghani poet and writer who lives in London. Since leaving Afghanistan in 1979, he has worked on humanitarian aid projects in Cambodia, Vietnam, India, Pakistan, Yugoslavia, the United Kingdom, and other countries.

Finally the plane touched the ground and along with many other passengers I saw the sunshine of my birth country after more than 20 years of leaving Kabul. My heart was beating with excitement and as soon as my feet were on the ground I went on my knees to kiss the ground. I had been missing the taste and smell of the soil of my country since childhood.

The idea of coming back was to work with a humanitarian organisation for the purpose of contributing to the reconstruction efforts. I never had the chance to go back earlier, first because of the Russians and then Mujahideens [Islamic warriors] and recently the [Islamic fundamentalist former rulers of Afghanistan the] Taliban. But this time it was different or at least that is what I was told. I wanted to see my country governed by the people who really wanted to serve. I wanted to see a great change to what was during the Soviet Union supported government, the Mujahiddeen and the Taliban. I went there with an open mind. I went there to be receptive to the ideas of developing my country with others who share the same goal.

Just some days after arrival I decided to go around and explore the city of Kabul. Etched were fond memories of this historical city, which had made me so impatient to see it again, and I had been waiting for the time when I could go back. Nostalgia. So there it was Kabul. The city that Babar the [sixteenth-century] Mughol emperor had been so in love with. The poets wrote poems of it and the travellers admired it. That was of course a long time ago but at least in my time, Kabul was wearing the proud dress of history with its museums packed with evidence of the glorious era, its libraries full of books, its archives alive and its university of high repute. Alas I saw nothing resembling my memories. Kabul in complete ruin, this is what I went back to.

Fundamentalists Still Rule Afghanistan

At the end every square metre of Afghanistan was painful. The Rulers in power in Afghanistan are still fundamentalists preaching through the voices of Mullahs who wake up early in the morning shouting at the people using their noisy loudspeakers criticizing those Afghan men for allowing their daughters to go to schools and their families to watch TV. Ironically Afghan TV does not offer anything especial. Women singers are not allowed to perform and there is nothing entertaining or educational, but cheap-censored Indian films and speeches by strict politicians capturing the TV screen, day in and day out.

"Every square metre of Afghanistan was painful. The Rulers in power in Afghanistan are still fundamentalists."

Outside, the streets are full of beautiful and vulnerable children of both sexes begging along with the disabled old men and women. Yet ministers are zooming with big cars from here to there. Every thing is just acting like a play away from reality. The warlord system is evident in all aspects of life. Mullahs with long beards demand to have bigger organisations and outfits supported by the international and UN [United Nations] funding. Having bigger organisations has nothing to do with reform and development but just to consolidate more power, more wealth and having more and more people under their control. It is nothing to do with employment generation as well. Because employment is only provided for family, friends or people of the same clan and party. If you are none of these then, you simply do not exist.

Horrifying stories become alive and they touch you, torture you and traumatise you. The story of [Afghan warlord and criminal] Zardad, who had a man-eating dog who was indeed a man. The story of [Northern Alliance warlords] Hezbe Wahdat eye gauging and cutting women's breasts. The stories of raping women and keeping them naked in cellars of the houses. The story of [warlord] Sayaf's [Ittehadi-Islami, Islamic fundamentalist] party hammering nails on the scalp of innocent civilians. The stories of destruction beyond recognition. The stories of madness, madness and madness. And of course the story of sadness because the same mad people are in power again.

Horror Stories Proliferate

Some of the stories like this I am relating, would appear in novels of most imaginative writers and the people would think it is fiction. But actually these are the true stories of Afghanistan. One story goes that there was a mad commander with long dirty and greasy hair who nourished lice on his head and who would routinely block the road with his bandit group demanding money from the travellers in the most unusual way. He would stop people and ask them to buy his lice, starting conversations like, "hey brother give me the palm of your hand" and the person stopped by the authority would oblige by stretching out his palm. The commander would put one of his lice on the palm of the traveller's hand. The traveller watches with disgust but cannot react knowing the commander would shoot him if he does not do whatever the commander wants. And the commander would authoritatively say "so tell me how much you pay for this healthy lice?" And if a reply was, "sir I do not want to buy it", the commander would roar, "You do not want to buy my lice? You stupid idiot, what is wrong with my lice? Buy it or I kill you."

The commander therefore sold the lice to the passers-by for a huge amount of money. The traveller keeps the lice only for a short distance controlling his disgust and when confident that the commander is no longer watching, he would throw it away, only to be stopped a short distance later by the commander and be interrogated further. "Hey what did you do with

> *"Now what is more shocking is the monopoly of power. In the eyes of Allah they are all equal but some are much more equal than others."*

my lice?" the commander would shout. "I threw it away sir". "Did you really?" "Yes". "You did very wrong you idiot. I think that I sold my lice for such a small sum to you. You have cheated me to agree to give it to you for almost nothing. Now you either return my lice or pay ten fold more."

Warlords Monopolize Power

And now what is more shocking is the monopoly of power. In the eyes of Allah they are all equal but some are much more equal than others. No doubt that there are a number of ministers not belonging to the Northern Alliance, but the power of these ministers is only symbolic. While I was there until September of the year 2002 the Minister of culture Mr Makhdom had no authority over the Chief of Kabul Radio and Television. While Mr Makhdom encourages the participation of women in radio television, the Chief of Radio, a fundamentalist Northern Alliance fighter, ignores that and issues his own home-made fatwas [religious decrees] and no women singer or artist performs on radio or television. Another story relates the prevailing culture, the story unfolds that in the past a man became the King of Afghanistan. The new king distributed power among his friends and his friends became ministers and governors. Unfortunately one of his very close friends was forgotten by the new king. The close friend complained bitterly that he did not have a significant post in the new king's administration. The king laughed and said, my dear friend you will be my watchman. Your job title may be watchman but you have my permission and power to slap the face of any minister that upsets you. There are so many watchmen like these in the new regime. The most powerful are those from Panjsheer [in northeast Afghanistan]. Don't be a minister but be a watchman from Panjsheer. That job is more powerful.

Aid Organizations Exaggerate Achievements

There are some signs of optimism such as seeing girls and boys going back to school. I travelled to Bamyan and was astonished to see my people still living in the dark caves. I was even more surprised to see the same people sending their children to schools. They know that most of the atrocities that happened in the country were related to lack of knowledge and education. UNICEF [United Nations Children's Fund] had predicted that only 1.5 million children would get back to school but the reality was much more optimistic with an estimated figure of some 4.5 million children attending schools by the summer of 2002. However, such an Afghan cultural revolution is not all successful because the enthusiasm of the people is not matched with the government's support. UNICEF and the government of Afghanistan have had the capacity perhaps to provide no more than very basic facilities for perhaps 50% of the 1.5 million targeted school children. Some remote areas such as Bamyan do not get any support. The schools that have been damaged are not repaired. Even UNICEF massages its figures by claiming that the organisation has rehabilitated a thousand schools. The reality is that much of UNICEF's engagement is cosmetic and for the sake of statistics, such as counting simply the replacement of a single door or minor repair in the name of reconstruction or in the more successful project cases the building of five classrooms for an area which require at least thirty-two. By manipulating the reality such organisations show in the release of their public information that they have single-handedly managed to meet most of the educational demands in Afghanistan, but the truth is different. Moreover, the warlords of the country do not allow the teachers to get their salaries. Teachers' salaries paid by the UN does not reach them. The warlords control provinces and warlords fraudulently retain the salaries. Teachers are powerless and have not received their salary for a long, long time in a system with no accountability.

Disturbing Social Inequities

I am deeply worried for the welfare of our children. There are a large number of children on the streets. Child labour is also very common. Children abuse cannot be ignored when there is extreme poverty. I have seen beautiful girls and boys begging on the street. I have seen children collecting food from garbage. I have seen children being chased by the new regime police and beaten up.

Social problems are ignored by the mullahs [clerics] supported by Mujahideen. I was there when a bomb planted in a car killed more than 30 people, including three brothers who were the sole breadwinners of a big family. For many days I was listening to the mullahs to hear any word of condemnation but there was none. The mullahs were delivering speeches on qurbani (slaughter) of animals in Eid [Islamic festival marking the end of the fast of Ramadan]. I found life to be so cheap in my country.

Afghanistan has a few new-rich people. There are streets in Wazir Akbar Khan, the most looked after area of Kabul which now belongs to Northern Alliance ministers. Fahim the defence minister has bought the whole street and blocked it for his own safety. His soldiers would not allow any body including pedestrians to walk on that street. Each of those houses at least has a value of 400,000 dollars. Thanks to Fahim and his friends destroying much of Kabul and maintaining only select areas of Wazir Akbar Khan and Shehre Naw, has forced the value of the houses upwards

> *"The reality is that much of UNICEF's engagement is cosmetic and for the sake of statistics."*

even to the extent of being more expensive than England. The lions of Panjsheer know very well how to get rich from wars. Yes destroy half of the country then, confiscating some houses from their owners in those parts that are not destroyed. That is the way to become rich. Becoming rich like this does not require qualification. Becoming a minister in Afghanistan does not need qualification either.

Women Still Denied Basic Rights

Whatever is considered to have been changed, one thing that has not changed at all is the rights of women. Muslim extremists do not recognise the rights of women. In my office where I was working women came to the office with fear. Their fear was not in their imaginations. People like [Afghan warlord] Gulbuddin Hekmatyar are there to throw acid on the faces of those women who appear on the street wearing modest chador but not burqa (veil). One of my female colleagues wanted to go to another country for training provided by the UN. The day she went to the passport office was one of her worst humiliating moments, this in the hand of a fundamentalist mullah who was in charge of the passport processing. He simply told the woman that she was a prostitute to be working in an office. However, being a prostitute and begging on the streets is not a problem. The extremists love to see poverty. They were the same people who sold the Afghan women to Arab fundamentalists. People still talk about the shameful act of [the] Taliban when they went and destroyed all Shomali [north of Kabul] killed men and took all the women, put them in buses and sent them to Pakistan where the Arabs on the other side received them. Where was the Afghan nang (honour)? Where was their Islam spirit at that time? It shows clearly that Islam has been misused by the Taliban and by the Mujahideen. It is a self-made Islam for protecting the interest of uneducated and backward extremists. It is not the real Islam.

Afghan Poor Are Victims of U.S. War

Life is very cheap in my country. Frustrated Americans who have failed to find [terrorist leader] Osama [bin Laden] or the real [international terrorist group] al-qaeda, bomb the wedding parties. I read the reports on the internet but no action is taken visibly or otherwise, by anybody to stop these crimes. I hear that it is the Northern Alliance guiding the Americans to bomb the Pushtoon villages. I just feel sorry for my people and then again, I know very well the stories of the Americans bombings in Cambodia and in Vietnam. The Americans are not in Afghanistan because they love the Afghans. They are there for their own interest and they use the Northern Alliance who has a very poor human rights record. The American humanitarian support to Afghans is the bombing of poor villages. Their record shows heavy spending in Afghanistan but not for the construction of schools and hospitals. It is mainly their war efforts. [Ronald] Reagan is back again in Afghanistan in the disguise of [George W.] Bush. His cowboys this time do not fight the Russians but the al-Qaeda. Who is paying for it is simply the poor Afghan masses. I know that Osama is going to emerge again in a different form and name, discretely supported by the USA. I know that, don't we all.

> *"It is a self-made Islam for protecting the interest of uneducated and backward extremists. It is not the real Islam."*

The turbans have changed to pakols [Afghan winter wool hats], but the heads are covered with the same mentality. The headgear is there not to allow the old fundamentalism to evaporate. My country's fall has not slowed or changed but only the appearance. The beards are trimmer, but the smell of fanaticism coming from unwanted hair is very strong indeed.

Afghan Women's Lives Have Not Improved

by Mariam Rawi

About the author: *Mariam Rawi, who is writing under a pseudonym, lives in Kabul and is a member of the Revolutionary Association of the Women of Afghanistan (RAWA), the most active women's rights organization in Afghanistan.*

When the US began bombing Afghanistan on October 7, 2001, the oppression of Afghan women was used as a justification for overthrowing the [Islamic fundamentalist] Taliban regime. Five weeks later America's first lady, Laura Bush, stated triumphantly: "Because of our recent military gains in much of Afghanistan, women are no longer imprisoned in their homes. The fight against terrorism is also a fight for the rights and dignity of women." However, Amnesty International paints a rather different picture: "Two years after the ending of the Taliban regime, the international community and the Afghan transitional administration, led by President Hamid Karzai, have proved unable to protect women. The risk of rape and sexual violence by members of armed factions and former combatants is still high. Forced marriage, particularly of girl children, and violence against women in the family are widespread in many areas of the country."

Continued Abuses of Women

In truth, the situation of women in Afghanistan remains appalling. Though girls and women in Kabul, and some other cities, are free to go to school and have jobs, this is not the case in most parts of the country. In the western province of Herat, the warlord Ismail Khan imposes Taliban-like decrees. Many women have no access to education and are banned from working in foreign NGOs [nongovernmental organizations] or UN [United Nations] offices, and there are hardly any women in government offices. Women cannot take a taxi or walk unless accompanied by a close male relative. If seen with men who are not close relatives, women can be arrested by the "special police" and forced to undergo a hospital examination to see if they have recently had sexual intercourse. Because of this continued oppression, every month a large number of girls commit suicide—many more than under the Taliban.

Women's rights fare no better in northern and southern Afghanistan, which are under the control of the Northern Alliance. One international NGO worker told Amnesty International: "During the Taliban era, if a woman went to market and showed an inch of flesh she would have been flogged; now she's raped."

> *"Every month a large number of girls commit suicide—many more than under the Taliban."*

Even in Kabul, where thousands of foreign troops are present, Afghan women do not feel safe, and many continue to wear the burka [head and body covering] for protection. In some areas where girls' education does exist, parents are afraid to allow their daughters to take advantage of it following the burning down of several girls' schools. Girls have been abducted on the way to school and sexual assaults on children of both sexes are now commonplace, according to Human Rights Watch.

The Government Does Not Protect Women

In spite of its rhetoric, the Karzai government actively pursues policies that are anti-women. Women cannot find jobs, and girls' schools often lack the most basic materials, such as books and chairs. There is no legal protection for women, and the older legal systems prohibit them from getting help when they need it. Female singers are not allowed on Kabul television, and women's songs are not played, while scenes in films of women not wearing the hijab are censored.

The Karzai government has established a women's ministry just to throw dust in the eyes of the international community. In reality, this ministry has done nothing for women. There are complaints that money given to the women's ministry by foreign NGOs has been taken by powerful warlords in the Karzai cabinet.

The "war on terror" toppled the Taliban regime, but it has not removed religious fundamentalism, which is the main cause of misery for Afghan women. In fact, by bringing the warlords back to power, the US has replaced one misogynist fundamentalist regime with another.

The US Supports the Warlords

But then the US never did fight the Taliban to save Afghan women. As recently as 2000 the Bush administration gave the Taliban $43m as a reward for reducing the opium harvest. The US supports the Northern Alliance, which was responsible for killing more than 50,000 civilians during its bloody rule in the 1990s. Those in power today—men such as Karim Khalili, Rabbani, Sayyaf, Fahim, Yunus Qanooni, Mohaqiq and Abdullah—were those who imposed anti-women restrictions as soon as they took control in 1992 and started a reign of terror throughout Afghanistan. Thousands of women and girls were systematically raped by armed thugs, and many committed suicide to avoid being sexually assaulted by them.

But lack of women's rights is not the only problem facing Afghanistan today. Neither opium cultivation nor warlordism and terrorism have been uprooted. There is no peace, stability or security. President Karzai is a prisoner within his own government, the nominal head of a regime in which former Northern Alliance commanders hold the real power. . . .

In November 2001 Colin Powell, the US secretary of state, said: "The rights of women in Afghanistan will not be negotiable." But the women of Afghanistan have felt with their whole bodies the dishonesty of such statements from US and British leaders—we know that they have already negotiated away women's rights in Afghanistan by imposing the most treacherous warlords on the people. Their pretty speeches are made out of political expediency rather than genuine concern.

Women's Group Supporters Are Persecuted

From 1992 to 2001 Afghan women were treated as cattle by all brands of fundamentalists, from jihadis to the Taliban. Some western writers have tried to suggest that this oppression has its roots in Afghan traditions and that it is disrespectful of "cultural difference" to criticise it. Yet Afghan women themselves are not silent victims. There is resistance, but you have to look for it, as any serious anti-fundamentalist group has to work semi-underground. The Revolutionary Association of the Women of Afghanistan (RAWA), which was outlawed under the Taliban, still can't open an office in Kabul. We still can't distribute our magazine *Payame-Zan* (Women's Message) openly. Shopkeepers are still threatened with death for stocking our publications, and RAWA supporters have been tortured and imprisoned for distributing them. People who are caught reading our literature are still in danger.

> "*US and British leaders . . . have . . . negotiated away women's rights in Afghanistan by imposing the most treacherous warlords on the people.*"

Feminism does not need to be imported; it has already taken root in Afghanistan. Long before the US bombing, progressive organisations were trying to establish freedom, democracy, secularism and women's rights. Then, western governments and media showed little interest in the plight of Afghan women. When, before September 11, 2001, RAWA gave footage of the execution of Zarmeena [a woman publicly executed by the Taliban], to the BBC, CNN, ABC and others, it was told that the footage was too shocking to broadcast. However, after September 11 these same media organisations aired the footage repeatedly. Similarly, some of RAWA's photographs documenting the Taliban's abuses of women were also used—without our permission. They were reproduced as flyers and dropped by American warplanes as they flew over Afghanistan.

Returned Afghan Refugees Live in Dire Conditions

by Ilene R. Prusher

About the author: *Ilene R. Prusher is a staff writer for the* Christian Science Monitor.

Bibi Hanifa lives in the skeleton of a building, where an unforgiving wind rushes down from the snow-capped Hindu Kush [mountain range in northeast Afghanistan] and meets no resistance. Her home, the abandoned headquarters of Kabul Power and Water, has no doors or windows, its dark and cold structure resembling in some ways a dark cave.

Encouraged to return to Afghanistan after the fall of the Taliban [Islamic fundamentalist regime] two years ago, [in 2001] the "former" refugee and her family soon found themselves homeless.

Save for a few blankets, bags of food, and pocket money they received from the United Nations when they crossed the border from Pakistan 1½ years ago, they say they have received no assistance.

I walked into Ms. Hanifa's world here a year ago, and sat shivering on the skinny floor cushions. I wondered how any family could survive here.

I soon learned that they had just buried an infant, Bibi Hanifa's niece. The family blamed it on the bitter weather. They were living in one room with no electricity, no heat, no plumbing, and no access to schools or healthcare. Despite their dire needs, help from aid agencies was not reaching them.

Hanifa was my immediate favorite. She had the startling khaki green eyes that only Afghans seem to have. She said she could not offer tea because of Ramadan [the Muslim fast], but she began to talk.

She told me she was ashamed of herself. She had brought up her eight children on dreams of returning home, and now they were angry with her for bringing them here. Their only hope, she said, was to scrape together enough money to go back to Pakistan for the winter.

Chapter 2

The Situation Is Deteriorating

At the time, I told Hanifa that with so much international aid pouring into Kabul, assistance was available—it might just be a matter of tracking it down. I gave her suggestions of places to look for help, and left, thinking it would only be a matter of time before conditions improved.

Now, a year later, I am the one who feels ashamed. Little has changed in Karta i-Seh, a neighborhood of southwest Kabul with so many collapsed buildings that it almost looks as if an earthquake had struck. Hanifa says things are getting worse because assistance is scarce—and Afghanistan is no longer a central focus.

"Last year was better, because at least they provided us with some coal and blankets," she began to talk. says. "This year we got nothing."

Hanifa struck me as beautiful last year. Today, she looks nearly a decade older. But her 3-year-old daughter has hardly grown and her hair looks more like an infant's than a toddler's.

"Last year, the foreign people were paying attention to us, but this year, they don't even ask if we need help," says Hanifa. "They said they would provide us with windows and doors, but nothing came and they never came back."

I ask who "they" were, but no one in the family is literate, rendering the workings of foreign-aid groups, the UN [United Nations], and the Afghan government a mystery to them. The only visitors in the past three months have been from a government ministry. They came to inspect the site and said they would evict the squatters and reclaim the land for Kabul Power and Water. They haven't returned yet.

I was drawn here because this is a part of the city that the world sometimes takes notice of, and yet quickly forgets. The families of Kart i-Seh saw some of the city's most devastating fighting [between rival ethnic groups] during the 1990s. Most here now are refugees—about 2.5 million of whom have returned to Afghanistan since the fall of the Taliban. Not all are happy they made the trip. The families here say they were better off while living in Iran and Pakistan, and many dream of going back. And UNHCR, the United Nations High Commissioner for Refugees, has pulled foreign staff out of a wide belt of southern and eastern Afghanistan after a French citizen was shot dead in Ghazni [in east Afghanistan] last month.

"Despite their dire needs, help from aid agencies was not reaching them."

Several billion dollars are supposed to be going to Afghanistan's reconstruction. At the UNHCR office in Kabul, an official tells me the aid organization has supervised the construction of 40,000 homes for refugees, mostly in rural areas, and that it will build another 60,000. But only 1,500 of them will be in Kabul itself, where most of the returnees have come in search of work and services. "The goal is to get people to return to their places of origin," says

Nadar Farhad of UNHCR. "We're focusing on the rural areas."

The current trend, it seems, is to give construction materials to refugees and encourage them to build their own homes. But that works only for rare refugees who own a plot of land in the crowded capital.

Returned Refugees Receive No Assistance

Farida Anwari is among the many who don't. Around the corner from Bibi Hanifa, past the bombed-out, rusting military vehicles which serve as jungle gyms for the children, Ms. Anwari's mud hut looks more like a mound of packed earth with an entrance than a house.

Inside, her home comes alive with pictures of movie stars and models. The shiny pin-ups contrast with the drab earthen walls, with twigs poking through like veins.

These pinups are what Anwari's uncle, Mohammed Issak, sells to survive: pictures of Indian movie stars, Japanese models, and blond children who transport the imagination far from the mud hut with no electricity.

Anwari once lived more comfortably. Her husband, a government officer, was killed in a rocket attack in the early 1990s. Afterwards, she fled to Pakistan with her four children, whom she supported by working as a maid. When the new Afghan government of Hamid Karzai took over in late 2001, she says, word spread: It was time to go home.

> *"Things are getting worse because assistance is scarce— and Afghanistan is no longer a central focus."*

"That's why we decided we should come back to our country," says Anwari, whose round, girlish face is framed by an bright orange scarf. Arriving in Kabul, Anwari found that her old home was destroyed. Desperate for shelter, she came here. With even the abandoned buildings overflowing, they had nowhere to live. Her uncle, also widowed in the war, helped her construct the mud house and moved in.

"When I came from Peshawar [in north Pakistan], I was very hopeful that the government would find a home for us. And the other hope was that I could get the children into school and I would work," says Anwari. "When I came, I found absolutely nothing." She can't find work, and says she can't get her children enrolled in schools because she has no money for fees. "I don't care about my life now, but I care about my children. If I could find work, I would spend it on their education."

If it weren't for her uncle's business, they wouldn't have enough to eat. Each day, Mr. Issak piles his pictures, stickers, and plastic flowers onto a wooden stand and carries it to a busy commercial district. There, he sells his goods to earn maybe 50 afghanis a day—about $1. Lately, he says, Taliban-type fundamentalists have been harassing him, telling him that his business, with its racy pictures of midriff-baring actresses, is an affront to Islam.

"They yell at me, 'Why are you selling these pictures? You'd be better being a pimp,'" complains Issak. He's been beaten several times, he says, by local police. "I tell them I'm doing this to support my family," he says. "If someone would give me a job, I'd do anything."

They've been to UNHCR several times to ask for help. They received only a tent to put over the hut. Anwari hopes that, and perhaps some distributions of coal or wood, will get them through the winter.

> *"People still living in Pakistan ask me, how's the life in Kabul? ... I tell them, don't go. Don't return to your homeland."*

Allah Nazar lives on the floor of a building where the ceiling is half collapsed, giving the children a round-the-clock view of the traffic below. Until recently, he was out working. But a cement mixer fell on his hand; he lost a finger and damaged several others. It is not clear if he'll be able to do manual labor again.

"To whom should we go? I don't know anymore," says Nazar, whose face is etched by deep lines. "We keep going to complain but they don't care." He fears officials will return to eject them.

"They said we should leave the building because they're going to start work here. And I said, 'Well, you'll have to kill all of us and our families first, because we have nowhere to go,'" he says.

"People still living in Pakistan ask me, how's the life in Kabul?" he says, and shakes his head. "I tell them, don't go. Don't return to your homeland. Can you imagine saying that?"

Chapter 3

Should the United States and the International Community Continue to Play an Active Role in Afghanistan?

Overview: A Debate on International Involvement in Afghanistan's Reconstruction

by Tariq Ali and Mike O'Brien

About the authors: *Tariq Ali is a British commentator on Islamic affairs and author of* The Clash of Fundamentalisms: Crusades, Jihads, and Modernity *and* Bush in Babylon: The Recolonisation of Iraq. *Mike O'Brien is the minister for trade, investment, and foreign affairs for the United Kingdom. In this viewpoint, they discuss the aftermath of the 2001 war in Afghanistan.*

Tariq Ali: The aim of the war and occupation was to capture and kill [the terrorist leaders] Osama bin Laden and Mullah Omar and shackle [the terrorist group] al-Qaida. The result has been a dismal failure. The video earlier this year [2003] of Osama and his deputy wearing their Chitrali hats [traditional Afghan hat] and strolling cheerfully in the Hindukush [in northern Afghanistan] was a cheeky reminder that on this front the war has been a dismal failure.

Removing the [Islamic fundamentalist] Taliban from power was always a secondary aim. The condition of the population is certainly not better today than before the war. The reconstruction has turned out to be a joke. The women's liberation talked about so eagerly at the time by the first ladies of [U.S. president George] Bush and [U.K. prime minister Tony] Blair has come to nought. More money is being spent on feeding and housing Western troops than on the war-weary citizens of Afghanistan. And it will end badly, just like the Soviet intervention did in the 80s. I fear another civil war is waiting in the wings.

Mike O'Brien: So scathing, so cynical, so wrong. When I drove through the suburbs of western Kabul, every building I passed had been damaged by 20 years of civil war. You impressively described those wars in your book, *The*

Clash of Fundamentalisms: Crusades, Jihads and Modernity.

But I saw a lot of people in those derelict homes making bricks and rebuilding. They were building because they had hope that the future could be better. I talked to people who were so glad that the Taliban were gone that they had tears in their eyes: women who no longer had to wear the burqa [robes] and who could send their daughters to school. I went to a school for the blind to present the children with some braille machines because Taliban had destroyed them all. "Failure," you say. It's not what they say.

Those who opposed intervention in Afghanistan would have denied hope to these people. But you are right on one thing. There are still mega-problems. There are drug warlords and poverty and injustice. There are terrorist incidents. The government needs the ability to better enforce its writ outside Kabul.

Yes, it will take years to sort out the mess created over decades. But there is today a hope that defies any hard-bitten cynicism. Those people impressed me with their determination to rebuild. [Afghan president Hamid] Karzai is an ordinary man trying to do an extraordinary thing, to create a democracy from devastation. There are no guarantees that he will succeed, but we should do all we can to help. The UN [United Nations] and the world have not turned their back. There is a lot of money going in there. Rebuilding will be hard and will take time, but it is worth it.

Ali: You sound like a Pravda [Russian newspaper] man I argued with in the early 1980s. He too accused me of cynicism when I denounced the Soviet intervention as something that would end badly. In reality the Russians did push through an effective modernisation in the towns that provided an educational system for all (including women), and the number of women working in schools and hospitals multiplied rapidly. That was the time when [U.S. president Ronald] Reagan and [British prime minister Margaret] Thatcher welcomed the bearded mujahideen [Islamic holy warriors] and introduced them to the western media as "the equivalent of our founding Fathers". They certainly were the founding fathers of the Taliban.

I doubt whether the current bunch can do anything that remotely resembles the Soviet modernisation. How can western regimes busy dismantling the welfare state and privatising everything at home create a social democratic paradise in Afghanistan?

The burqa is back in business, I'm afraid, enforced by the men who rule

> *"The reconstruction has turned out to be a joke."*

the country with Washington's blessing. Human Rights Watch has spoken to women who said they veiled themselves to avoid violence and harassment. Add to that the fact that ministers are busy demolishing homes (possibly not the ones you visited) to grab land, and that senior Afghan military commanders and officials are involved in corruption and violence on a daily basis. This is reality for the majority of Afghans.

Chapter 3

Minimal Reconstruction

There has been little reconstruction. Very little of the $4.5bn (£2.7bn) pledged in Tokyo [at the international aid donor's conference] in 2002—a pittance even then—has come through. The World Bank estimates that a minimum of $13bn is needed to reconstruct the country. It was no problem finding $11bn to fight the war and occupy the country, but it's virtually impossible to raise funds to repair the infrastructure. This is the pattern of all the recent wars. In most cases, foreign interventions create more problems than they can solve. The western states act usually to defend their own interests.

As for poor Hamid Karzai, he is a longtime worker for the US intelligence agencies, like his friend [US special envoy to Afghanistan] Zalmay Khalilzad who put him there. But he seems to represent nobody inside Afghanistan. I fear he might be bumped off despite the all-American bodyguard.

There are two choices. Either he could be put on a Paris catwalk to model shawls, or the Dear Leader [British prime minister Tony Blair] could find him a safe New Labour [Party] constituency [in the United Kingdom]. It would be mean-spirited, having used him as a filter, to let the brutes of the Northern Alliance [group of US-backed Afghan warlords] flush him down.

O'Brien: I doubt that many Afghans would share your charitable view of Soviet occupation. But let's not let political prejudice get in the way of the facts, eh? $4.5bn was pledged at Tokyo but you missed out that it was

> *"There is today a hope that defies any hard-bitten cynicism."*

pledged over 5 years, not all in one year. Much of that money is now flowing and will continue over the next five years.

Schools have opened, hospitals operate and a road is to be built from [the capital] Kabul to Jalalabad [in Nangahar province in east Afghanistan]. Some $1.8bn in foreign aid was spent last year and the UK alone provided £45.5m at the start of last year. We are committed to spending £322m over five years— £122 million more than we pledged at Tokyo.

Okay, so all this will not create a social democratic paradise. I think Afghans, like the rest of us, are prepared to wait for paradise if they could get peace and a reasonable standard of living now. And things are not as bleak as you portray. Four million children are now back at school, 37% of them are girls and the numbers are rising; eight million children have been vaccinated against measles, preventing 30,000 deaths; over six million children have been immunised against polio; and more than two million refugees have voted with their feet and returned to Afghanistan because they now have hope. In addition, more than 400,000 internally displaced persons have also been able to return home.

Not paradise, but Hamid Karzai will not have to go looking for New Labour constituency. He will have a few remarkable achievements to put before his own people in the presidential election due in 2004.

Ali: My only point about the Soviet occupation was that, like Washington, they believed their modernising reforms would do the trick. Now the arguments you deploy are virtually the [same]. The difference is that the Russians did achieve much more. Incidentally, the figures you supply are already being challenged by all sides. Many refugees who went back have returned to Pakistan. Law and order does not exist, not even in parts of Kabul.

> *"In most cases, foreign interventions create more problems than they can solve."*

The barons of the Northern Alliance control the country and are biding their time. That's why I would urge you again to get Karzai out while you can. He would make a good politician in this country [England]. . . .

The imposition of a puppet regime, propped up by Nato [North Atlantic Treaty Organization] troops, thousands of miles away from base, is untenable. It might have helped to build the image of the Dear Leader as a War Leader (". . . grave, not grandiloquent . . . sincerely moved . . . this emotional fluency is wonderful gift in politics, especially at times of war," gushed [reporter] Philip Stephens in the *Financial Times*). But no amount of cluster-bombs and daisy-cutters can solve the problem.

Very few Afghans support this occupation. Sooner or later you'll have to pull out the Marines. Then what? A Northern Alliance bid for power and a new forward thrust by the Pakistan army. This time their boys will be clean-shaven and attired in modern dress. It could go down well on the networks and Fox TV. The modern soldiers of our closest ally sweeping the bearded men of the Northern Alliance out of the way and retaking Kabul. It could happen.

I hope, Mike, that you will soon emerge as the leader of the anti-war faction in New Labour. . . . In reality, and I'm quite serious, I think you should resign from the government and use your talents to win the party over for the future. New Labour will probably win the next election, but it has already lost the argument.

O'Brien: Thanks for your email and your solicitations for my future. I will stick with this government and this government will stick by the Afghans in reconstructing their country.

You attack my figures with vague references to challenges from "all sides". Name them, I say!

You use the fact—which I readily agree with—that there are problems in security. But to suggest what? That we should leave Afghans to another civil war? Perhaps we are the anti-war faction in Afghanistan now.

Like [pessimistic character] Private Fraser in [the British television comedy] Dad's Army you seem to say: "We're all doomed!" I accept that we need to tackle the security problem. Some 300 British troops are doing just that, alongside Germans, Canadians and others. Provincial reconstruction teams have recently been established to address the problems of the warlords. For the first time in 23 years there is a government and an army which is representative of all Afghans. We must continue this work.

And it is not just idealism. 90% of the heroin in Britain originates in Afghanistan. The security problem means opium production will go up before it comes down, but if we stick with it and eliminate poppy growth by 2013 we will have helped both Afghanistan and Britain. We are funding the Afghans to produce sustainable crops to eat and sell instead of poppies. We cannot create paradise there but we can help reduce the suffering.

By the way, if the Afghans don't want Karzai—the current choice of their traditional parliament, the Loya Jirga—then in 2004 they can vote him out. Votes, not bullets, I say!

Ali: It will not work. First, because there is no representative government (even in the broadest sense of the term) in the country. And I would urge you not to treat the Loya Jirga as anything but a collection of tribal leaders who are bought in the open market.

The Foreign Office where you sit has all the documentation. The British empire played the same tricks for over a century. The fact that your chum Karzai is a puppet of Washington is hardly a secret.

The 2004 "elections" will be just like the ones the British empire pushed through in Iraq during the early colonial period. What that produced according to a subsequent British intelligence assessment was "an oligarchy of racketeers".

Idealism, my dear Mike, has nothing to do with any of this. The Afghan adventure was a crude war of revenge. The fact that Europeans are involved doesn't make it any better. If New Labour intends new colonisations then these should be openly discussed and argued. They didn't work before. Why should they now?

As for the figures, just look at the Human Right Watch reports on refugees and women. They are lying on my desk in London and I'm sending this last one from New York. Or follow the time-honoured . . . method: type out Google.com, write "Afghan Refugees" and then see what hits the fan.

On the crucial question of your own future and that of Karzai, let's continue to talk. I am concerned.

O'Brien: You present no alternative policy, merely rhetorical fireworks, sparkling but fleeting. As a minister I have to work out how Britain can help the Afghans to reconstruct their country.

> **"Things are not as bleak as you portray."**

The era of colonialism is dead and any western leader who does not realise this is a fool. The west cannot run Afghanistan but we must empower the Afghans to run it for themselves, then we must get our troops out. Our best long-term guarantee is a genuine democracy in Afghanistan.

Yes, the Loya Jirga wasn't perfect but it was the best we could do at the time.

Next year's election will be better. The measure is whether things are improving, not whether they are perfect.

At least we are looking to give the Afghans all the help they need. Tony Blair promises it and we are delivering. The figures I quoted are real British taxpayers' money flowing to help the Afghans.

The difference remains that my responsibility as a minister is deliver, while your responsibility as a writer is to criticise. My record will be measured in the improvements in the lives of Afghans, yours in influencing public opinion about [the] Labour [Party in the United Kingdom].

I still believe government driven by idealism can do good things, you don't. So I will get on with helping the Afghans and you will keep on knocking our policy. Even so, I enjoyed our exchange—a bit of healthy criticism can improve ministerial performance!

Continued Support for Afghanistan by the International Community Is Vital to Global Security

by Ishaq Sharyar

About the author: *After the fall of the Taliban in Afghanistan in 2001, Ishaq Sharyar renounced his American citizenship to return to serve his native land as Afghanistan's ambassador to the United States from 2001 to 2003. He continues to work for the reconstruction of his country.*

Editor's Note: The following viewpoint was originally given as testimony before the U.S. Senate on June 12, 2002.

I would like to begin my remarks with a simple observation—and to present —context for this hearing [U.S. Senate Foreign Relations Committee hearing in 2002 on the Afghanistan Freedom Support Act].

The observation. The Official Name of my Country is "The Transitional Islamic Republic of Afghanistan." "Transition" is a key phrase and umbrella theme for my remarks this morning.

We are a work in progress—and in a context—the context of history and the context of regional instability.

Two decades ago a very bright professor named [Zbigniew Kazimierz] Brezinski [foreign affairs adviser to the Kennedy and Johnson administrations in the 1960's], referred to our region in the Middle East—the north and west side of the great mountains that divide Asia from Europe—As the *"Arch of Instability."*

But in recent years—without question, that arch has become a Circle of Instability—matched by an arch that extends across the southern and eastern side of the mountainous continental fence—and includes Pakistan, India, Bangladesh and even as far as Indonesia.

Ishaq Sharyar, statement before the U.S. Senate Foreign Relations Committee, Washington, DC, June 12, 2002.

At the center of this circle—is Afghanistan. Afghanistan is at the center of to-day's "Circle of Instability."

But this is not new. It is history repeating itself. For 4,000 years, Afghanistan has been a "portal" for history . . . more than just a crossroads . . . a portal.

For all of human history, overland travel from Europe or the Middle East to Asia could only pass one way—through Afghanistan—and through the Kyber Pass.

Ghengis Kahn [twelfth-century leader of Mongol Empire], Tamerlane [fourteenth-century Mongol con-queror of Afghanistan and northern India], Alexander the Great [second-century B.C. king of Macedonia, who conquered Persia, India, and Egypt],

> *"If the Western World has a lapse of attention and turns elsewhere, . . . a weak Afghanistan . . . will turn back toward terror and conflict."*

to name a few—crossed Afghanistan and left their mark on Afghan government, arts and sciences.

Others, of course entered and occupied Afghanistan as well—but left behind only destruction and chaos. In our generation, it was the Soviets in the 1980s, and the Taliban of the 1990s.

I offer this brief history lesson—to suggest the following:

Afghanistan is literally the "*high ground*" of history.

Control the Afghanistan high ground, and you will influence for good or for evil—that which flows into Europe and into Asia.

If the Western World has a lapse of attention and turns elsewhere, the "institu-tional memory" of the region will leach back in to a weak Afghanistan with drugs, corruption, and terror—and invariably—"the circle" will turn back to-ward terror and conflict.

If the Western World sustains support—and stays focused and present until democracy and prosperity are firmly rooted—then Afghanistan will become a hub—a hub of wheel of regional stability, democracy and prosperity—that will become self-sustaining.

Analogy with Macedonia

This is not theory, it is a replay of another recent and successful deployment of U.S. and international will on a smaller scale—where foresight was acted upon—indeed the foresight of this Committee was acted upon—and conflict on a broad scale was essentially prevented.

I invite you to compare the regional geopolitical situation of land-locked, im-poverished—but historically significant Afghanistan in the Middle East and Asia—to that of land-locked, impoverished—but historically significant—*Macedonia*—in the Balkans.

As you know from history—Macedonia in many ways is the historic portal that connects Europe and the Middle East—in the same way that Afghanistan is the portal that connects Asia and the Middle-east.

There, in Macedonia, for the first time ever—The U.S. and NATO [North Atlantic Treaty Organization]—very smartly—deployed a military presence BEFORE conflict spilled into that historic tinderbox.

Yes, there have been flashes of conflict in Macedonia—as flashes of conflict continue today in Afghanistan. But that historic "Center of Balkan instability" was made secure and regional conflict was avoided—a conflict that might have brought two NATO powers to blows.

The analogy of that successful—and modest investment—holds for Afghanistan and the current Circle of Instability in the Middle East.

Consider the following comment from Ahmed Rashid writing in the *Far Eastern Economic Review* in an article titled: *A Desire to Be Left Alone*—with a tagline:

> "Afghanistan's power-hungry neighbors threaten to revive the ruinous civil war of the early 1990s that gave rise to the Taliban.

> "Russia is arming one warlord, Iran another. Wealthy Saudis have resumed funding Islamic extremists and some Central Asian Republics are backing their ethnic allies. India and Pakistan are playing out an intense rivalry as they secretly back opposing forces. The playing field is Afghanistan, and the interference threatens to revive a multifaceted power struggle that in the early 1990s eventually gave way to a near-ruinous rule by the Taliban."

This is pretty straight talk.

It doesn't get more concise in describing the cycle of the 1990s—and what could re-emerge—OR—can clearly be prevented if the U.S. and world community remain invested in the security and rebuilding of Afghanistan.

Perhaps it is a stretch to ever envision Afghanistan as a "Switzerland of the Middle East." But I find it useful to think in those terms.

We must begin with the premise that Afghanistan, like every other sovereign nation—is for the Afghan people—AND NOT the playing field for regional rivalries. And we must begin with this premise and hold firmly to it.

Democracy Will Work in Afghanistan

The institutional memory in the region that reaches back 4,000 years. And regrettably that institutional memory favors dictatorship over democracy—and economic suppression over economic prosperity.

And the bad habits that go with that history also include devoting resources to developing nuclear, chemical, and biological weapons to enforce repression—at the expense of economic opportunity and prosperity for people.

Look at Iran and Iraq—two countries blessed with immense petroleum wealth—where people live in poverty.

Repression is a medieval concept—that does not belong in the 21st century.

• The denial of personal liberty removes transparency in government that leads to corruption.

- Corruption repels investment and economic development.
- Poverty is the soil where terrorism takes root—and makes the whole process of democracy, stability, and security impossible.

Now—I know that I am preaching to the choir here.

These concepts are second nature to you. But they are novel—if not radical concepts to the 100s of millions of people in the Middle East and South Asia.

> *"Poverty is the soil where terrorism takes root—and makes the whole process of democracy, stability, and security impossible."*

I have heard some say that openness and democracy conflict with our Middle Eastern culture and tradition.

Nonsense.

It was Cyrus the Great of Persia who issued the world's first declaration of human rights.

Yes, there have been periods of greatness in the Middle East. But to date, the ancient cultures have failed to translate themselves into modern times, because there has been no one to lead beyond the past—with the knowledge and convictions that—

- Theocracies fail;
- Dictatorships fail; but
- Democracy—somewhat more cumbersome to implement—works.

But I believe, however, that the cycle of history in Afghanistan is being broken by leadership with a new vision.

The people of Afghanistan have rallied to President Hamid Karzai as the one person who is truly able to unify Afghanistan, and turn the nation from a past filled with war and repression—to a future focused on prosperity and democracy.

A Long Way to Go

We began our future last year [2001] with liberation—and with the restoration of our spirit. For a country that has literally been reduced to rubble—it is our creative spirit and our culture that anchors our new beginning.

To be frank—there is little else in our country that will hold an anchor.

With liberation—we've had the opportunity to reclaim our culture—our art, our music, our educational systems, our entrepreneurship—our freedom to create was given back to us. The grays and blacks imposed on us by the Taliban—are being replaced by color.

- Our men can again play music.
- Our women and girls are returning to schools.
- And our children can again fly kites.

You've seen these things on CNN. You also know that we have a long way to go:

- 1 in 5 children born today will not reach the age 5 years;
- 1 in 10 Afghan women will die in childbirth—leaving her other children as orphans;

- Of Afghanistan's 27 million people—the United Nations estimates nearly a quarter are refugees; and
- Afghanistan is the most heavily mined country in the world. And as is the case in other war zones—children at play, will become the victims of left-over land mines.

Addressing the humanitarian issues, the security issues, the rebuilding issues, and the economic development issues are not simple.

It has meant an international collaborative effort—and to date, this multinational collaboration is working—and working better than perhaps any comparable effort since the Marshall Plan [to help reconstruct Europe after World War II]. . . .

Afghanistan's Progress

I think we have made great progress. Here is the testimony of Robert Oakley, former U.S. Ambassador to Pakistan in a recent Op-ed from the *Washington Post:*

"Starting from zero a year ago, the administration of President Hamid Karzai has achieved many attributes of a responsible government.

• It has a long-term national development framework and budget, worked out with the World Bank, the United Nations, the United States and other donors, and is carefully applying it to ensure that donor proposals meet Afghan realities.

• A central bank, fiscal discipline and a new national currency have been established.

Construction of the large-scale "ring road" program has begun; large-scale community development projects will soon follow smaller efforts.

• An Afghan Defense Commission (including senior 'warlords') has reached agreement on the size, makeup and training of the new army and the demobilization of local militias."

Ambassador Oakley goes on to say what I firmly believe:

The key to this trend line continuing in a positive direction—is the continued presence and focused attention of the United States of America.

The American effort has already been heroic, creative, and generous. Consider, just in recent months:

> *"To date, this multi-national collaboration is . . . working better than perhaps any comparable effort since the Marshall Plan."*

- The Congress and Administration produced the $3.3 billion Afghan Freedom Support Act;
- [U.S. State Department] Secretary Powell unveiled the Administration's U.S.-Middle East Partnership Plan; and
- The President dispatched a special delegation of American women to Kabul under the auspices of U.S.-Afghan Women's Council

But this trend line of attention and active support must continue into 2003.

If it does—and I believe it will—the good news will continue and Afghanistan will become the first example in this new century and centuries to come—of what democracy can do for a struggling nation. . . .

International Support for Security Is Crucial

Afghanistan internal security remains fragile. Recent outbursts of fighting . . . reminds us of the specter of oppression and terrorism that was only too real 18 months ago.

Non-interference from our regional neighbors is key. And the expansion of ISAF [International Security Assistance Force] and the establishment of a national army will:

- demonstrate international support for the *central government*
- *weaken* the influence of regional leaders and their personal armies
- *speed reconstruction* and economic recovery
- increase the confidence of *private investors*
- will promote stability and our ability to form a *national army*

Afghan Army needs to be trained at a faster pace and bigger size. 2000 men in one year are just not enough. Experts say that at least 700,000 guns are unaccounted for and it takes a strong army not only to collect them but also to counter the warlords. And their rapid deployment along with U.S. forces would not only make them better soldiers but also amount to smaller number of casualties of U.S. armed services.

> *"Afghanistan will become the first example in this new century . . . of what democracy can do for a struggling nation."*

The expansion of ISAF, is very good for all of the Afghan people—who have known only war for the last generation.

The expansion of ISAF—will also help finish the job of extinguishing all vestiges of the Taliban and Al Qaeda in Afghanistan—so democracy has a chance—good for the Afghan people AND the global community.

To that end—it is critical even in these times of global economic slowdown—that Afghanistan receive the promised security and financial assistance to help Afghanistan to recover, and rebuild. . . .

Karzai Government Programs

The Karzai government has organized with remarkable speed and transparency [the rebuilding of Afghanistan]. And we are making progress against a very long checklist. Here are highlights:

- We have implemented a plan for efficient processing of economic development assistance—housed in the Ministry of Finance—under a program that would make the Director of OMB [the U.S. Office of Management and Budget] proud.

- We have introduced our new national currency—the Afghani.
- We have embarked upon a highway "ring-road" reconstruction program to build arteries connecting a country the size of Texas. Additional road building will begin with the arrival of spring [March 2003].
- The Voice of America and the Afghan Information Ministry, with $10 million from the Pentagon, are installing transmitters to create a national radio network.
- Also with America's help, through Transition Initiatives funding in the amount of $6 million, we are empowering Afghan-run NGOs [nongovernmental organizations] particularly focusing on women's groups and community development projects. We want to make sure that women are full participants and full beneficiaries in the economic growth that is part of Afghanistan's future.

I believe that with the restoration of civil society and the rule of law—the international private business community will see a welcome mat for business and private investment. And in recent months, we have begun reaching out to the private business and financial communities—with an invitation to come and do business.

Indeed—this is the mission I have personally embraced in my role as Ambassador. We have great wealth in our undeveloped natural resources in Afghanistan. But we also understand that international businesses will not invest and joint-venture with us until they see:

- a safe environment,
- the banishment of corruption,
- adherence to commonly accepted business practices, and
- re-establishment of reliable transportation and telecommunications infrastructure.

And with the generous support of international institutions and the U.S. we are working hard to bring these things to pass.

We have the basic elements for building wealth in our nation,

- We have Natural resources—and they need to be mapped and thoughtfully developed;
- We are located in a strategically important location in Central Asia—much like Denver, there can be a logistics and transportation industry in our future;
- And we have an entrepreneurial tradition . . .

but these elements will never be organized and mustered—independent of peace and security—and the establishment of a civil society.

Economic Development Plan

Security and Economic Development—are the two rails of our track toward the future.

Better security paves the way for businesses and investment.

Businesses provide freedom with jobs, money for education and personal empowerment—and more opportunities for women.

We know where we want to be—and here is part of our strategy—our business plan—to get there.

I have helped to create the Private Sector Development Task Force for Afghanistan. It is a

> *"It is critical even in these times of global economic slowdown—that Afghanistan receive the promised security and financial assistance to help . . . [it] to recover."*

- Coalition of private companies, non-governmental organizations and volunteer experts—dedicated to accelerating the development of a private enterprise-driven market economy in Afghanistan.
- The primary goal of the Task Force is to promote capacity building and institution building of the Afghan government and strengthen infrastructure.
- We are working with the Ministry of Justice to create laws that will protect private investment.
- We are setting up private banks.
- We are working with the U.S. Geological Survey and private energy companies to explore our natural resources.
- We are bringing in the most recent and cost-effective telecommunications technologies—and a new license for a new wireless company was just recently let.
- And later this year, we will host an international trade show in Kabul and YOU—are hereby invited to attend.

When you arrive, just tell them Ishaq sent you.

It will be good for top accommodations—not 4 star . . . yet. But . . . one with relative luxuries—a beautiful carpet on the floor—and reliable electric power.

Long-Term Commitment for Afghanistan

In closing, I hope I have offered a useful assessment of where we are and where we hope to go.

I must be candid—we are not there yet, by any means. And if the progress that we have made in the past year or so is to continue, we will need help—financial help, technical assistance, and a certain amount of patience.

But I will say again, should not be viewed as altruism by the U.S. or world community. The returns to the U.S. and global security will be commensurate with the investment.

And I will also tell you that President Karzai and I are passionately determined not to squander this moment in Afghanistan's 4,000 year history.

Afghanistan has had enough political revolutions.

Afghanistan has been invaded and occupied by the armies of soldiers.

What we need today is to be occupied by a new benevolent kind of army: an army of teachers, doctors, builders, farmers, civil engineers, merchants, bankers and public safety experts—and perhaps even a few lawyers.

The goal here is a jump-start. Not a permanent occupying force. And many of you here in this room—are in many ways part of this benevolent army.

We all need to make sure that the work undertaken on behalf of rebuilding Afghanistan is done in a manner which empowers the people of Afghanistan to take matters into their own hands.

As the Afghan proverb says, "A river is made drop by drop." Any great project, any important human undertaking, takes time and requires a long-term commitment. Clearly, the rebuilding of Afghanistan after more than 20 years of war and foreign occupation will take sustained effort and patience. And the timing is urgent.

Afghans are also a remarkably resilient people and a proud people—proud to learn; proud to do a good job.

As [former British prime minister Winston] Churchill wisely stated, "Give us the tools and we will get the job done."

The International Community Must Help Afghanistan Establish Peace

by Kofi Annan

About the author: *Kofi Annan of Ghana is the seventh secretary-general of the United Nations. He was appointed by the UN General Assembly to his first term in that position in 1997 and reappointed for a second five-year term in 2002.*

Editor's Note: The following viewpoint was originally given as a message to the International Conference on Afghanistan in Berlin on March 31, 2004.

You are meeting at a time of cautious celebration. Since the [aid donors'] conference in Bonn nearly two and a half years ago [in 2001], Afghanistan has achieved remarkable progress. This is due primarily to the determination of the Afghan people not to allow the country to slide back into civil war.

Through two Loya Jirgas [people's assemblies], and now during the preparation for the electoral process [for the 2004 election] the people of Afghanistan are showing—in their country's finest tradition—their willingness to work together and to move forward. They have demonstrated remarkable patience, as the new State, which they so dearly wish to see up and running, becomes better equipped day by day to control insecurity and expand reconstruction.

Another crucial factor has been the strong partnership between the Afghan Government and the international community—a partnership that has flourished since the signing of the Bonn Agreement and the first donors' conference in Tokyo in 2002. It has shown the Afghan people that they are not alone in their struggle to put a definitive end to decades of conflict—and thus bolstered their hope that they will ultimately succeed.

The Bonn process now faces one of its major challenges—the holding of a free and fair election. So far, the registration process reflects the clear desire of Afghans in all regions and all walks of life to join in the political process. And

Kofi Annan, statement before the International Conference on Afghanistan, Berlin, Germany, March 31, 2004.

the expected outcome—a fully representative government—will undoubtedly mark a decisive step in the democratic transition, and thus make a major contribution to the consolidation of peace.

Yet the magnitude of the election task is enormous. Objectives that have eluded us for two years must now be achieved in a very short time, in particular:

- Greater security to allow registration and polling to take place everywhere in a balanced manner;
- Greater political freedoms for all competing parties and candidates, including the possibility of organizing openly and safely, with access to the media; and
- Demobilization and reintegration, which, since the signing of the Bonn Agreement, have been the single most pressing demand from the Afghan people, irrespective of their political and ethnic background. In advance of elections, this will be essential in order to clear the political arena of all factional militaries and to allow for political party activity to be carried out in accordance with the new constitution.

> *"The strong partnership [with] . . . the international community . . . has shown the Afghan people that they are not alone in their struggle to . . . end . . . decades of conflict."*

Only if these objectives are met can the election fulfil its potential as a tool for state-building and national reconciliation.

Security Assistance Needed

This ambitious agenda will put everybody to the test, Afghans and international community alike—and perhaps nowhere as much as in the field of security. This conference provides an invaluable opportunity for the Afghan Government and international community to agree on the benchmarks that will need to be met to achieve credible elections. Security assistance remains one of the most important contributions—if not the most important—that the international community can make.

The recent outbreak of violence in Herat, which resulted in the death of Minister for Aviation and Tourism and perhaps as many as 100 others, is a deplorable example of the terrible impact that the factional rivalries which beset Afghanistan can have. The disarmament, demobilization and reintegration of ex-combatants, the reforms of the national security sector, and international security assistance are all vital if we are to bring an end to this factionalism and build lasting stability based on truly national institutions.

The people of Afghanistan, after a prolonged war, still suffer from continued insecurity from terrorism, factionalism and lawlessness, and still dread the possibility of a return to conflict. I trust that you will seize the opportunity of this conference to give them the firm, long-term commitment they are looking for.

A successful election would be a fitting culmination of the efforts of the past two years to bring security, good governance and reconstruction to Afghanistan. The authority and legitimacy of an elected government would boost the ability of the State of Afghanistan to address outstanding tasks, among them the daunting narcotics challenge. But it would still not be the end of the road that began in Bonn. Much of the work of building a fully functional State would still lie ahead. Creating the instruments of the rule of law is not a short-term undertaking. As I said in my report to the Security Council in March 2002, it will take more than 36 months to heal the wounds left by 23 years of war.

Afghanistan has a constitution unanimously approved by a Loya Jirga, and it will have elected institutions. But to complete its transition to peace and democracy, it will also need the continued assistance of the international community. The partnership which emerged in Bonn, and which has been strengthened through countless initiatives over the past 24 months, must continue until the transition is complete; until the State of Afghanistan can stand on its own two feet, equipped with effective and impartial security forces, respectful of human rights; a professional civilian administration; a functional justice system; and the ability to address the basic needs of its people.

This conference is a unique opportunity for the Government to reaffirm its commitment to that agenda, and for the international community to send the Afghan people an unequivocal reassurance that it will remain by their side.

The United States Must Aid Afghanistan in Order to Fight Terrorism

by Martin Ewans

About the author: *Martin Ewans, a British diplomat formerly based in Kabul, is the author of* Afghanistan: A New History.

Although Afghanistan won its independence from British control in 1919, it was not until a quarter century later that the Afghan and U.S. administrations, just about as geographically remote from each other as was possible, considered there was sufficient content in their official relations to an exchanging of diplomatic missions. Following World War II, Afghans were anxious to develop a relationship with what they saw as a strong, influential nation with sound anticolonial credentials, but they found themselves rebuffed.

Keen to obtain external assistance for their postwar development, they approached the United States in 1947 for help with an ambitious hydroelectric and irrigation project on the country's longest river, the Helmand. There was, however, little enthusiasm for the scheme in Washington, and it was left to a private U.S. company, Morrison-Knudson, to assist in its construction. Money soon ran out, and a request for a $120 million loan from the Import-Export Bank was whittled down to an inadequate $23 million. Essential surveys neglected or cut short, and relationships deteriorated. Salination and waterlogging compromised the project, dooming it, to a large extent, to failure.

From 1948 on, Afghanistan approached the United States for help in equipping and training its antiquated armed forces but was similarly cold-shouldered. In 1955, a final request was turned down by John Foster Dulles. This seemed odd in the context of his Cold War policy of constructing treaty relationships around the periphery of the Soviet Union and communist China as a safeguard against the spread of communism.

Although Afghanistan was well placed geographically as a buffer along the

Martin Ewans, "America and Afghanistan: A Troubled History: With the Soviet Withdrawal from Afghanistan in 1989, American Interest Quickly Lapsed, Even Though the Afghan Conflict Had Helped to End the Cold War," *The World & I*, vol. 17, March 2002, p. 20. Copyright © 2002 by News World Communications, Inc. Reproduced by permission.

Soviet Union's southern frontiers, it was politically at odds with Pakistan, a linchpin of the Central Treaty Organization. Unwisely in view of its landlocked position, Afghanistan had been supporting a movement among the Pashtun tribes for an independent state in the northwest region of Pakistan, contiguous to Afghanistan. Additionally, the United States was reluctant to incur any obligation to assist Afghanistan should it be threatened militarily by the Soviet Union. The country was felt to be too remote and exposed for any such guarantee to be successful.

Afghanistan Under the Soviets

The reasons for the United States not becoming involved were rational enough, but they effectively delivered the country into the hands of the Soviet Union. In 1955, Moscow hastened to supply Afghanistan with arms and military training, as well as a generous program of economic development.

After some delay, the Americans changed tack and decided that Afghanistan should not be left exclusively to the communist bloc, so they, too, went into the business of developmental assistance. Among other projects, the United States and the Soviet Union cooperated to build a strategic network of roads across the country (which later facilitated the Soviet invasion), while the United States also concentrated on assisting the University of Kabul and Afghanistan's national airline, Ariana.

It was fortunate for American interests, although not for Afghanistan itself, that during the 1960s and '70s, the Soviets proceeded to overreach themselves. An independent, nonaligned, but friendly Afghanistan, closely associated in their sphere of interest, would have suited them well, but they could not resist the temptation to engage in subversion.

Military personnel who went to the Soviet Union for training were routinely indoctrinated, while the Soviet Union also supported the People's Democratic Party of Afghanistan (PDPA), a party founded in 1965 that was, in all but name, the Afghan Communist Party. The first communist president of Afghanistan, Nur Mohammed Taraki, was financially assisted by Moscow, and his successor, Hafizul-

> *"The reasons for the United States not becoming involved were rational enough, but they effectively delivered the country into the hands of the Soviet Union."*

lah Amin, was almost certainly recruited by the KGB [Soviet Russia's intelligence agency] while doing postgraduate studies in the United States.

When, therefore, the PDPA mounted a coup in April 1978 and established a communist regime in Afghanistan, the Soviets found that they had created a monster they could not control. Although they had doubts of the wisdom of establishing a communist regime in a country as feudal as Afghanistan, they did nothing to prevent it.

U.S. assistance to the University of Kabul was also in some respects counter-productive, in that it became a hotbed of unrest, where many students, bitter at the lack of employment opportunities, were attracted to the Left. Of the 21 men who constituted the first PDPA cabinet, no fewer than 10 had been educated in the United States and a mere 3 in the Soviet Union.

Within its first few months, the Afghan communist regime had so antagonized the populace that uprisings and mutinies occurred across the country. Dominated by the dogma that a communist revolution, once it had occurred, was irreversible, the Soviet Union finally decided that the only option was to invade, which it duly did at the end of 1979.

> *"U.S. policy was to keep the Soviet wound bleeding by supplying . . . arms to the . . . [Islamic resistance], but not enough [support] to defeat the [Soviets]."*

Against all expectation, its forces encountered tough and sustained guerilla opposition. This soon necessitated decisions in Washington about the nature and extent of any assistance to the mujahideen, the "holy warriors" who formed the nucleus of resistance.

During the first few years, despite the suffering inflicted by the conflict, U.S. policy was to keep the Soviet wound bleeding by supplying sufficient arms to sustain the mujahideen, but not enough to defeat the Soviet occupation. The arms supplied were not American but clandestinely purchased secondhand Soviet armaments from such countries as Egypt and Israel (the latter had captured them during various wars in Arab states) that were shipped to the mujahideen via Pakistan.

Soviet Withdrawal

In April 1985 the policy changed when [U.S. president] Ronald Reagan issued National Security Directive No. 166, ordering the United States to use all available means to compel the Soviets to withdraw. Following this instruction, the CIA adopted two strategies, both highly risky, aimed at making life difficult for the Soviet occupiers.

The first strategy was to supply the mujahideen with 900 Stinger surface-to-air missiles, along with training in their operation. (Many of these missiles have never been recovered.) The second was to supply arms and training to Muslim resistance fighters in Pakistan.

Both strategies worked well. The Stingers hampered Soviet airpower, while the so-called Arab Afghans (none of whom were Afghans and by no means all Arabs) proved themselves not only committed but increasingly battle hardened. Their numbers eventually ran to at least 35,000 and, by some accounts, appreciably more. Among them was a young Saudi plutocrat, Osama bin Laden, who fought little himself but supplied finances, facilities, and, ultimately, leadership to the Arab Afghans from a base in Peshawar [in north Pakistan].

With the Soviet withdrawal from Afghanistan in 1989, international interest in that country quickly evaporated. The conflict had claimed the lives of one million Afghans. Though it had helped catalyze the dissolution of the Soviet Union and the end of the Cold War, this was an eminent case of there being no gratitude in politics. The survivors received little concern, although a large refugee population needed care. Agriculture and industry had been destroyed, and the countryside was booby trapped with millions of land mines.

The mujahideen were excluded from the negotiations leading to the Soviet withdrawal, and so there was no agreement on an acceptable postwar political settlement. Over several years they proceeded to compete for dominance, variously supported by Pakistan, Iran, and other neighboring states. Receiving little encouragement from the United States or elsewhere, the United Nations attempted some totally ineffectual mediation, while the scant humanitarian aid that was forthcoming was grossly inadequate for the country's needs.

Taliban Regime

The next chapter in the saga was written in 1994. By now disillusioned by its clients among the mujahideen, Pakistan switched its support to a new movement, the Taliban, whose rank and file, as well as leaders, were mostly the products of radical Pakistani religious schools. The majority of Arab Afghans still in the region were happy to join its ranks and fight what they saw as a continuing religious war.

Despite official denials, there is no doubt that the Taliban received military support from Pakistan and financial support from Saudi Arabia. There is also the question of American involvement. Although direct support has not been proved and is on the whole unlikely, the United States welcomed the Taliban's arrival on the scene, seeing it as opposed to Iran and believing that it would stabilize the country and the region. The United States also set store on the Taliban's undertakings to end Afghanistan's significant cultivation and trafficking of narcotics.

Above all, with the fragmentation of the Soviet Union, central Asian oil and gas fields were potentially important to the global market. A U.S. company, UNOCAL, actively sought to build a pipeline from Turkmenistan to the Arabian Sea through Afghanistan.

"From the outset . . . the U.S. record in Afghanistan has been one of purposelessness, ambivalence, and neglect."

However, Washington's optimism about the Taliban was soon shattered. It proved unable to extend its control over the whole country and so ensure sufficient security for a pipeline. Rather than suppress the drug trade, the Taliban proceeded to encourage it, to its own considerable profit.

In 1996 bin Laden was allowed to return to Afghanistan, where he trained and organized his Arab Afghans into an international terrorist network, aimed mainly against the United States and Saudi Arabia. The Taliban's brutal social and judicial policies, notably its treatment of women, aroused strong protest in the United States and elsewhere, effectively precluding a close relationship. Afghanistan under the Taliban became a pariah nation, left to suffer under a singularly repressive regime and a landscape that deteriorated during a prolonged drought. The Taliban threatened the stability of Pakistan (where it had enjoyed much sympathy), whose nuclear weapons would become a major threat to peace if they were to fall into the hands of extremists.

The Need for a Major International Effort

From the outset, therefore, the U.S. record in Afghanistan has been one of purposelessness, ambivalence, and neglect. It failed to prevent Afghanistan from coming under Soviet control and shunned it following the Soviet withdrawal, with the result that Afghanistan became ripe for the Taliban takeover. But its main error was in promoting the "Arab-Afghan" presence during the Soviet occupation. The moment of truth came in 1993, when it was found that the [first] World Trade Center bombers were Afghanistan-trained militants.

Bin Laden subsequently used his militants to mount murderous attacks on U.S. targets overseas and finally on the World Trade Center on September 11, 2001. Many of them have formed cells around the world, posing a threat to the stability of governments that are vital for U.S. global interests. Unraveling and neutralizing bin Laden's network will take years of effort and immense amounts of money.

> *"After years of neglect, a major international effort is an absolute necessity."*

Singularly lacking in U.S. policy toward Afghanistan have been consistent, long-term planning based on reliable intelligence, and an appreciation of its importance in the context of America's global interests. At this point, after years of neglect, a major international effort is an absolute necessity.

The main issue, however, is wider than that. The bin Laden brand of terrorism is the product of twisted minds and a subculture of religious fanaticism. Such fanaticism would not find a sea in which to swim but for a growing resentment, verging on despair, among the wretched of the earth. This is directed at a world order under which a minority, mainly in Europe and North America, live in unprecedented affluence, while the great majority, not only in the Muslim world but more widely, are compelled to live in abject poverty. It is unlikely to be a coincidence that Afghanistan, which is probably more wretched than any other country in the world, has also been the seat of a global terrorist threat.

The United States Should Not Pursue Nation-Building in Afghanistan

by Subodh Atal

About the author: *Subodh Atal is an independent foreign affairs analyst based in Washington, D.C.*

Two years after the [terrorist attacks] of September 11, 2001, and the subsequent defeat of the Taliban [regime in Afghanistan] and al Qaeda [terrorist group] by U.S.-led forces, Afghanistan remains highly unstable, and the U.S.-led war to rid the nation of Islamic extremists is faltering. According to numerous recent reports, the Taliban is regrouping, in partnership with al Qaeda remnants. Meanwhile, Gulbuddin Hekmatyar, a former Afghan prime minister and leader of the radical Islamic party Hizb-e-Islami, has called for a jihad [holy war] against foreign occupiers and the creation of an Islamic state. These groups are attacking Afghan government targets, U.S. and other coalition forces, and civilian reconstruction projects. Warlords continue to feud with each other, undermining Afghan president Hamid Karzai's regime, and they have resuscitated the narcotics trade. Karzai is secure only inside his own compound, and doesn't trust his own defense ministry troops to act as his bodyguards.

In this worsening environment, there are renewed calls for the United States to intensify its involvement in Afghanistan. A report by the Council on Foreign Relations and the Asia Society recommends an expanded U.S. peacekeeping role, billions of dollars in new reconstruction aid, and active support for Karzai in his disputes with Afghan warlords. The Bush administration revealed in late July 2003 that it would request an additional $1 billion in aid for Afghanistan.

Proponents of an increased U.S. commitment suggest that failed nations are potential hotspots for terrorist activity. In November 2001, Clare Short, then the British government's International Development Secretary, accused the United States of "turning its back" on the developing world, and she asserted that the alleviation of poverty worldwide was central to a global effort to fight terrorism. The United States has been admonished for "abandoning" Afghanistan after the Cold War, precipitating its descent into the Taliban-dominated era, and is now being criticized for not committing whole-heartedly to the nation's reconstruction following the war that ousted the Taliban. A recent report by Human Rights Watch chastised the U.S. government and other coalition partners for failing to restore order and security in the country, and called on the international community to rein in local and regional warlords and to expand peacekeeping operations.

This [viewpoint] examines various impediments to a wider U.S.-led reconstruction of Afghanistan. The security situation in Afghanistan is the biggest hurdle to such efforts. The nation is divided along ethnic lines, and feuding warlords further undermine the chances for sustaining a strong central government. The U.S. presence has already begun to trigger resentment and has even renewed sympathy for the Taliban in significant sections of the country. The Afghan situation closely parallels that of other countries where U.S. intervention failed in the past. Given America's prior experiences in similar situations, policymakers should refuse to widen the U.S. role in Afghanistan's reconstruction and focus instead on rapidly eliminating the anti-American forces that are resurgent in the region.

The High Cost of Nation Building

President Karzai's visit to Washington in February 2003 was aimed at refocusing American attention back on his nation despite the impending war on Iraq and the other crises occupying center stage at the White House. While speaking to the Senate Foreign Relations Committee, Karzai reported a long list of achievements including the return of refugees and increased control by his central government over Afghan provinces, and he requested increased U.S. involvement and funds in various Afghan reconstruction efforts. Several individuals representing a diverse spectrum of opinion, including Sens. Chuck Hagel (R-Neb.), Barbara Boxer (D-Calif.), and Joseph Biden (D-Del.), responded favorably to Karzai's call for increased U.S. aid.

Less than a month later, the United Nations Security Council outlined a series of high-level political goals for Afghanistan, including the creation of "a multi-ethnic, gender-sensitive and fully representative government," with elections targeted for June 2004. Apart from the building of political institutions, other major Security

> *"The Afghan situation closely parallels that of other countries where U.S. intervention failed in the past."*

Council goals that remain unfulfilled are enhancing internal security; disarming militias; countering the narcotics trade; building an effective, independent judiciary system; expanding human rights; improving health and education; and building critical infrastructure such as roads.

The costs of this ambitious set of goals are substantial. Michael O'Hanlon of the Brookings Institution estimates that between $15 billion and $50 billion is needed for the rebuilding of Afghanistan over a 10-year period and suggests that the United States provide at least 15 percent of the total aid to retain influence over "how the aid effort is administered and how the country is rebuilt."

"Assuming for the sake of argument," O'Hanlon continues, "a total annual aid package of $3 billion, the U.S. share might then be $400 million to $500 million." Over a 10- or 15-year period, such aid could total as much as $7.5 billion. As daunting as that figure seems (O'Hanlon offered his proposal in December 2001), the actual amount being spent in Afghanistan might already be much more. A report in the *New York Times* quoted unnamed American officials who projected that the cost in 2003 for operations in Afghanistan would likely equal the $935 million spent in the previous year. That figure did not include the cost of maintaining troops in the country and reflected expenditures on a number of civilian reconstruction projects including the building of roads and schools.

Other reports show American aid totalling more than $300 million, but it is not clear that this aid will be sustained at those levels for many years. The *Washington Post* reports that the $1 billion package proposed by the Bush administration in July 2003 is "designed to fund projects that can be completed within a year to have a maximum impact on the lives of the Afghan people" in order to boost the Karzai government prior to elections planned for October 2004.

> *"One of the first prerequisites for successful nation building is a stable security situation—the very condition that does not exist in Afghanistan."*

Lack of Security Sabotages Reconstruction

Notwithstanding past failures, many observers hold out hope that an American-led nation-building effort in Afghanistan will succeed. Such optimism ignores the fact that one of the first prerequisites for successful nation building is a stable security situation—the very condition that does not exist in Afghanistan. In the absence of a secure environment, nation-building efforts can get bogged down and eventually grind to a halt. Lebanon and Somalia are examples of situations in which external aid efforts were stymied by unresolved conflict and a lack of security. Combatants opposed to foreign intervention find it easy to sabotage reconstruction efforts, preventing civilian authorities and outside agencies from performing their tasks.

That is precisely what is happening in Afghanistan. In the words of Ramtanu Maitra [Indian engineer and journalist] of the *Asia Times*, "Afghanistan is not just dicey, but outright dangerous," and the situation there is hardly conducive to reconstruction. In this environment, an Afghan vice president was assassinated last year [2002], and Karzai himself survived an attempt on his life in September 2002. In late January of this year, hundreds of U.S. soldiers, backed by air power, attacked radical Islamic militants in the Spin Boldak area in the Kandahar district. Soon thereafter, a powerful bomb blew up a civilian bus, killing 18 in Kandahar. By April, the militants had regrouped and were carrying out new attacks on U.S. and Afghan government targets. Aid workers were also targeted. Suspected Taliban loyalists killed two U.S. soldiers in March 2003 in an ambush, and two other U.S. military personnel died in a firefight in April. In July 2003, a landmine planted by the Taliban killed eight Afghan soldiers.

> *"If a substantial part of Afghanistan remains under the grip of insurgents, the commitment of external resources—no matter how large—will be ineffective."*

The Afghan rebels have demonstrated an ability to regroup and return after U.S. operations temporarily drive them out of their strongholds. This is especially true in the eastern provinces. It suggest that the militants have support in the tribal areas bordering Pakistan, where Pashtuns dominate. If a substantial part of Afghanistan remains under the grip of insurgents, the commitment of external resources—no matter how large—will be ineffective.

Warlord Rivalries Threaten Recovery

Provincial and local leaders, better known as warlords, each backed by his own militia, have been the powerbrokers in Afghanistan since the days of the anti-Soviet resistance. The U.S. strategy of stabilizing Afghanistan following the collapse of the Taliban includes partnering with many of the warlords and securing their support for Karzai's central government. The warlords' agendas, however, do not parallel with those of the Americans. Many of the warlords have survived for decades through a combination of aid from external forces, their own ruthlessness, and a lucrative role in drug smuggling. The loyalties of these warlords are accordingly fickle, and they have little interest in supporting a strong central government that would encroach on their power.

Among the warlords who collaborated with U.S. forces to oust the Taliban is Abdul Rashid Dostum who controls the Uzbek-dominated territory around Mazar-e-Sharif. Dostum is funded by Uzbekistan, and may also be in the pay of Iran. Dostum's militia has clashed for control of northern Afghanistan with the forces of fellow Uzbek Mohammed Atta, and with those of Tajik [in northeast Afghanistan] leaders Burhannudin Rabbani and Mohammed Fahim. Those sporadic battles prompted the UN [United Nations] to suspend aid operations in July 2002. Rabbani, a former prime minister, has his own ambitions of coming back to power in Kabul and is reportedly trying to influence local commanders by bribing them.

In Herat, near the Iranian border, governor Ismail Khan has largely supported the United States but is reported to have connections to Iran, and has expressed impatience with the continued U.S. troop presence in the province. Khan's militia has clashed with that of a rival warlord, Amanullah Khan, who is reportedly supported by the Taliban. In this region, therefore, the United States faces an interesting dilemma, as it may be forced to choose between an Iranian-backed warlord and one connected to the Taliban.

Khan is challenged to the east by Gul Agha Sherzai. Sherzai's sphere of influence includes the provinces of Kandahar, Oruzgan, and Helmand, where the Taliban were strongest. Although Sherzai was "bought off" by millions of dollars in U.S. and British money, the amount was apparently not sufficient to deter him from clashing with rivals such as Khan.

Warlords Challenge U.S. Peace Efforts

In eastern Afghanistan, where infiltration across the Afghan-Pakistan border is a major concern, U.S.-led stabilization efforts also face considerable obstacles. Bacha Khan Zadran, whose militia operates in Khost and Paktia provinces, collaborated initially with U.S. Special Forces in the U.S.-led Operation Anaconda to drive out massing Al Qaeda fighters in March 2002. In return for his support, Zadran was paid nearly a half a million dollars. Having secured that amount, Zadran assaulted the Khost capital of Gardez, home to a U.S. base. The May 2002 rocket attack killed more than 30 civilians. Last fall, when U.S. forces asked Zadran to dismantle some checkpoints, rival leader Hakim Taniwal's fighters took it as a cue to attack Zadran's militia. Zadran, whose ambition is to rule over not only Khost and Paktia provinces, but also neighboring Paktika, has now turned against the United States. In March 2003, his militia attacked U.S. and Afghan government forces. In one of the clashes, Zadran's eldest son was killed, an incident that has only further alienated the warlord against the United States and the Afghan central government.

It is thus becoming increasingly clear that partnering with and bribing Afghan warlords is unlikely to accelerate the nation's recovery. The Soviets tried, and failed, to secure their hold on the country by buying the warlords' loyalty. The United States is experiencing a similar phenomenon.

Growing Anti-U.S. Resentment

Insecurity and infighting among warlords are not the only impediments to a successful nation-building effort in Afghanistan. One of the many perils of nation building is that, despite the best intentions and efforts of the foreign power, the local population starts to resent its presence. This phenomenon was evident in Iraq as early as April 2003, mere days after the fall of Baghdad. After Saddam Hussein's ouster, many Iraqis—including Shias [an Islamic sect] who had been suppressed by Hussein and who had been protected under the southern no-fly zone by the U.S.—turned against American troops. The anti-American feelings surprised the troops as well as America's wartime leaders. Americans are also surprised to learn that there is considerable resentment toward U.S. troops in South Korea, Japan, and Germany, where U.S. soldiers have been stationed for decades.

Many factors can contribute to such resentment, and each nation-building endeavor must contend with unique circumstances. Afghans have bitter memories of Soviet occupation and have traditionally resisted the imposition of foreign ideologies. In the past, once this resentment built above a certain threshold, the presence of the foreign power became a flashpoint for violent resistance, as happened to the Soviets after the first year of their military intervention. Going even further back in history, the first British invasion in 1838 was at first welcomed by some Afghans. However, resentment against the foreign occupation built quickly, especially over the clash of cultures between the occupation forces and local Afghans. Shah Shuja, the Afghan leader anointed by the British, was secure only under their protection, similar to Karzai's situation today.

> *"It is . . . becoming increasingly clear that partnering with and bribing Afghan warlords is unlikely to accelerate the nation's recovery."*

In the case of the U.S. presence in Afghanistan, several mitigating factors have slowed the development of massive resistance. Many Afghans opposed the Taliban and they fought side by side with American troops to expel the medieval regime. Those individuals continue to work closely with U.S. authorities. Other Afghans have simply tired of the incessant fighting, and they look hopefully for a chance for peace.

An initial welcome for foreign intervention can quickly turn into a deeply antagonistic relationship, however. In such situations, the presence of outside peacekeepers can become counterproductive. In Afghanistan, there are signs that resentment of the U.S. presence is building. Continued conflict, including U.S. operations against Al Qaeda, have killed and injured dozens of civilians. Notwithstanding the unfortunate accidents that have claimed civilian lives, the continued U.S. military presence also bruises cultural sensitivities. Afghan civilians have complained of raids on their houses by U.S. troops while women were present. Errant U.S. bombs in civilian areas, including one that killed 11 civilians in April 2003, have exacerbated an already tense situation. On May 6, 2003, the first large-scale anti-U.S. protests took place in Kabul.

Afghans Should Decide on Their Government's Structure

The bitter fighting among the various warlords and persistent foreign meddling have contributed to an ethnic fragmentation that cannot be readily overcome by nation-building activities. Ethnic tensions were clearly exacerbated during the period of anti-Soviet resistance when different factions were the beneficiaries of external assistance. However, the actual roots of those tensions are deeper. The British imperialists had a tough time keeping the region under their control and out of the Russian realm. The Afghan-Pakistan border is actually an artifact of

British colonial rule. In the face of frequent and nagging Afghan resistance, the British drew an arbitrary line—the Durand Line—which demarcated Afghanistan from imperial India, and divided the rebellious Pashtuns. Populations on either side have never accepted the division, and today the Pashtun tribes on the Afghan side have more in common with their brethren across the Durand Line than they do with the Uzbeks and Tajiks in northern Afghanistan.

Those persistent ethnic tensions are equally important today, as Afghans and outsiders attempt to shape the nation's future. The southern Pashtuns harbor significant resentment over the degree of control that the Tajiks, Uzbeks, and Hazaras of the Northern Alliance have over the Karzai regime. While considerable attention is being paid to the establishment of a strong central government as a milestone of Afghanistan's nation-building process, the lack of respect commanded by Karzai's central government and the de facto autonomy practiced in the warlord-led Afghan provinces suggests that other alternatives to nation building should be considered. Above all, policymakers should recognize that it is unwise for external actors, including the United States, to dictate the structure of the Afghan government. A centralized regime imposed from the outside will likely result in further resentment against the United States. Given the deep divisions within the country, a federal structure, with a considerable degree of autonomy granted to provincial leaders, may be the only practical solution—but that decision should be left up to the people of Afghanistan. . . .

Poor U.S. Record in Nation Building

To assess the future of American policy in nations such as Afghanistan and Iraq, U.S. officials would do well to look at history and consider the results of past interventions. A recent study by the Carnegie Endowment for International Peace estimated that out of more than 200 military interventions by the United States since 1900, only 16 were aimed at creating democratic institutions. Of those 16, only 2 countries—Japan and Germany—made the successful transition to stable democratic governments. Two other nations—Granada and Panama—are too small to be significant. In all other cases, there was no functioning democracy in place 10 years after the end of American involvement. It is impossible to predict whether there will be democracy in Afghanistan in 10 years; however, given the myriad aggravating factors in that country, including continued conflict, resistance to external meddling, and a cultural gap between western objectives and the traditional Afghan approach to problems, the prospects for successful nation building are bleak.

> *"In Afghanistan, there are signs that resentment of the U.S. presence is building."*

Nonetheless, there has been no shortage of calls for nation building. Much of this derives from the argument that terrorism thrives amidst poverty and political chaos. Susan Rice of the Brookings Institution classifies a large number of states as failed, failing, or "causes for concern" and suggests that the United States follow a policy of "early and aggressive" intervention in those nations. Her rationalization is that without early intervention such states act as hosts to terrorist groups, trigger regional conflagrations, and ultimately require far greater resources in terms of conflict resolution and peacekeeping. However, many of the nations that Rice characterizes as either failed or failing—such as Somalia, Sierra Leone, and Cote D'Ivoire—do not serve as significant hosts of terrorist groups. On the other hand, terrorist groups such as the Irish Republican Army and the Basque separatists have operated for years in the United Kingdom and

> *"Policymakers should recognize that it is unwise for external actors, including the United States, to dictate the structure of the Afghan government."*

Spain, two nations that can hardly be considered candidates for nation building.

Rice also fails to consider that foreign intervention often has unintended consequences, and may even result in wider regional conflict, as happened in Afghanistan itself during the 1980s, or in Southeast Asia in the 1960s. She does consider the costs of exacerbated regional tensions and weapons proliferation that could be incurred by the United States if it doesn't preempt state failure, but she ignores the cumulative cost to the United States of "early and aggressive" intervention in what may amount to dozens of countries around the world. Such a policy is questionable in any era, but it is especially so today, when American military forces are already strained to the breaking point as they police the sprawling American empire. More importantly, the tremendous drain on resources from nation-building exercises provides little value to national security, a security that appears shakier today, following the events of September 11, than it did at the end of the Cold War.

Numerous Calls for Nation Building

Rice is not alone in her calls for preemptive nation building. In 2002, Sen. Chuck Hagel sponsored a $3.3 billion program for economic, political, humanitarian, and security assistance for Afghanistan over four years. Less than three months after President [George W.] Bush signed the aid package into law. Hagel was back for more, calling for still more money for Afghanistan to create stability and prosperity. Sen. Barbara Boxer is even more ambitious, calling for the expansion of International Security Assistance Force operations to areas outside Kabul because "women face harsh restrictions under local leaders." Such calls ignore prior lessons in Afghanistan, where the imposition of a foreign ideology by the Soviets only served to deepen resentment by locals who then focused their attention on hastening the end of the foreign occupation.

Sen. Joseph Biden has been one of the most vocal supporters of nation building in Afghanistan, calling for an Afghan Marshall Plan [which was implemented to help reconstruct Europe after World War II]. However, the Marshall Plan analogy for Afghanistan is inappropriate. Local conditions contributed more to Europe's recovery from the Second World War than did Marshall Plan aid. The total amount of aid never amounted to more than 5 percent of GNP in the Marshall Plan countries, and there is no data to suggest that this aid was instrumental: Belgium's post-war recovery was the fastest in Europe even though the Belgians received a relatively small share of Marshall Plan money, the British, on the other hand, received the most aid, but had the slowest rate of economic growth in post-war Europe. Economic freedom, respect for private enterprise and entrepreneurship, and the rule of law are the key elements of growth and prosperity. Foreign aid is often counter-productive to these ends.

Simply put, there does not appear to be a positive correlation between the extent of economic and political intervention and the ability of outside forces to shape a nations's destiny. The recent Council on Foreign Relations–Asia Society task force report recommends increased U.S. intervention in the Karzai-warlord disputes and an enlarged role in Afghanistan's reconstruction, ostensibly to prevent the nation from slipping back into anarchy and again becoming a terrorist haven. But the longer the United States and other foreign governments remain in Afghanistan, the greater the likelihood that their efforts—notwithstanding their noble intentions—will be seen as an attempt to subvert the will of the Afghan people. An extended American presence therefore will create an atmosphere conducive to supporting the very terrorist elements that presence is intended to eliminate.

America Should Focus on Eliminating Terrorists

Afghanistan was freed from Taliban rule approximately 18 months ago. Since then, attacks by Taliban loyalists, al Qaeda remnants, and renegade warlords have undermined fledgling reconstruction efforts in the nation and exposed the Karzai regime's lack of control outside Kabul. Karzai has pressed the Bush administration for an expanded commitment to the rebuilding of Afghanistan, and many observers, including some in the U.S. Congress, have seconded his calls.

However, a number of factors in Afghanistan, and past experiences in nation-building exercises around the world, suggest that pumping resources and effort into reconstruction in the absence of security and economic order will not have the desired outcome. An increased U.S. commitment to civilian reconstruction may only distract us

> *"The tremendous drain on resources from nation-building exercises provides little value to national security."*

from the goal of eliminating anti-U.S. Islamic extremists who will sabotage any rebuilding efforts. Although much of the focus to date has been on empowering a strong central government in Afghanistan, deep ethnic fissures and the persistent strength of the regional warlords suggest that such an aim is too ambitious.

The U.S. military forces currently operating in Afghanistan should concentrate on smashing the Taliban and al Qaeda remnants who are regrouping along the Afghanistan-Pakistan border. Once this goal is achieved, U.S. forces need not remain in the nation. Following the end of military operations, the focus could then shift to monitoring Afghanistan and its neighbors to ensure that forces that threaten the United States are not resurrected. Most of this work can be conducted by U.S. intelligence services in cooperation with our allies in the region.

"The United States abandoned Afghanistan after the Cold War," was a common refrain heard after the September 11 attacks. Indeed, the national security threat that was incubating in Afghanistan since the mid-1900s was ignored at a grave cost. A preemptive move against al Qaeda and the Taliban, and their allies, might have headed off the threat that culminated in 9-11. However, it is far from clear that sustained nation building by the United States after the Soviet withdrawal would have been successful in the 1990s or would even be feasible today.

Involvement in Nation Building Detracts from Hunting Terrorists

In the aftermath of the disastrous Soviet attempt at nation building in Afghanistan, any peace enforced at the point of the gun would have served to turn many of the mujahadeen [Islamic warriors] factions against the United States. The U.S. military would have had to take sides in the competition among the irregular forces led by the likes of Burhannudin Rabbani, Ahmed Shah Masood, Rashid Dostum, Gulbuddin Hekmatyar, and Ismail Khan. A similar attempt to interpose American troops between competing warlords following a Soviet withdrawal from an impoverished country met with an unfortunate and embarrassing end, and the situation in Afghanistan is far worse than the one encountered in Somalia in 1993. Furthermore, given the intense rivalry among neighboring powers over influence in Afghanistan, a long-term military presence could well have enmeshed the United States in regional quagmires such as the India-Pakistan conflict and confrontation with Iran. Instead of recrimination, instead of replaying the errors of the past, U.S. policy toward Afghanistan in the 21st century should focus on the known threats that still operate there.

Lessons from prior experiences in nation building can be applied beyond Afghanistan to a broader policy framework. A blanket policy of early and aggressive intervention in overseas hotspots is likely to be counterproductive and costly. Although the United States cannot afford to ignore national security threats in the post 9-11 era, neither can it afford to get entangled in the innumerable conflicts and tensions around the globe, risking distraction from the crucial goals of hunting and eliminating America's enemies.

The American Infidels Must Get Out of Afghanistan or Risk Catastrophic Consequences

by Gulbuddin Hekmatyar

About the author: *Afghan warlord Gulbuddin Hekmatyar, the founder and leader of the radical Islamic fundamentalist party Hezbi Islami, has repeatedly called on Muslims worldwide to wage jihad (holy war) on the American "infidels" in Afghanistan. From 1993 to 1994 Hekmatyar was Afghanistan's prime minister.*

I am writing this letter to you on behalf of the oppressed Afghan nation about the war-mongering policies of American President, [George] W. Bush, which if not stopped will entail irreparable loss and catastrophic consequences for the whole world in general and for the Americans in particular. We, Afghans, draw your attention to some important aspects of this ravaging war:

The American unjust and illegal aggression against Afghanistan, the ruthless genocide of civilians, blind aerial bombardment of towns, villages, mosques, and imposition of a corrupt and despotic minority with a dark history of war crimes are the main reasons for the deep hatred and hostility of Afghans against the Americans. This hatred has gradually led to an armed resistance.

The people saw that the Americans are not only enemies of [the Islamic fundamentalist group, the] Taliban and [terrorist organization] al-Qaeda, but they are also antagonizing every Afghan mujahid [Islamic warrior] and Muslim. They insult the Afghans on the pretext of searching their homes and looking for weapons. They are supporting and protecting those groups which are old allies of the Russians.

On the contrary, they arrest rivals of pro-Russian groups, accusing them of collaboration with Taliban; detain them in their bases or summarily dispatch

Gulbuddin Hekmatyar, open letter to President George W. Bush, the Democratic Party of the USA, and its members in the Congress, October 2002.

them to [American detention camps in] Guantanamo [Bay, Cuba]. People see that the Americans are acting as if they are conquerors of Afghanistan and must rule it with an iron hand. They are out to apprehend, crush and wipe out all those people and forces in Afghanistan which believe in freedom and independence of their country; demand that foreign forces should desist from meddling in their internal affairs and want that the Afghans must be left to decide their future and solve their problems amongst themselves.

This insulting and humiliating conduct of American troops with the Afghans, even if tolerated by other nations, can never be tolerated by the freedom loving Afghans who are proud of their dignity and independence. Afghans prefer to die honourably but never accept to lead an undignified life. They can tolerate the trials and tribulations of life but cannot reconcile even with the concept of subjugation by foreigners.

Americans Violate Traditions

Haven't you read about the story of the proud Afghan woman whose gate was crushed by the searching team of American troops. The Afghan lady asked the intruding soldiers not to enter the house as there were no male members of the family present at home, but the arrogant American 'cowboys' did not pay any heed and crushed her gate. Infuriated by this blatant arrogance and insulting behaviour, the proud Afghan lady grabbed the family gun and shot at the American 'elite.' Dumbfounded commandos, not able to put a dignified fight against a lonely Afghan lady, beat a hasty retreat and sent an SOS for help. The village was besieged by other troops, and F-16's and B-52's, the last resort of the cowards, appeared in the sky.

The American commander demanded that the Afghan lady be surrendered to them, threatening to raze the village to the ground in case of defiance. But the people of the village defiantly responded that they were ready to face the challenge but would never commit such a disgraceful act, blaming the Americans for violation of the Afghan traditions by forcefully entering a house in absence of the male members of the family. They said they were ready to sacrifice their lives and property in defense of their religion and honour.

Is it not shameful that the American need F-16's and B-52's to fight against an Afghan woman? This is the real picture of your war in Afghanistan, as

> *"Foreign forces should desist from meddling in their internal affairs and [leave the Afghans] . . . to decide their future."*

you are fighting ordinary Afghans who are not Taliban and have no links whatsoever with al-Qaeda. They are only defending their lives, their honour and dignity and their freedom and religion. Even if they cannot put a challenge to your high-altitude bombers they can repeat the feats and heroics of this Afghan lady. The story of this lady and hundreds of similar feats should have proved to you that permanent occupation of Afghanistan and ruling this country of freedom loving people by force is only a dream which will never come true even for the fiercest aggressors despite all their modern technology and weapons.

Deceiving the American Public

Unfortunately, the Bush regime and army generals involved in the war in Afghanistan have been able to keep the American nation in total darkness, painting a rosy picture of the events in Afghanistan and repeating lies after lies. They are trying hard to make the Americans believe that their troops are greatly welcomed in Afghanistan, being received with open arms and bouquets of flowers. It is astonishing to see that there are no sane voices to question these blatant lies; to say: Is it possible for a nation whose 25000 defenseless citizens have been brutally murdered to welcome the murderers of their sons; love the killers of their beloved ones; and receive with flowers those whose hands are red with the innocent blood of their near and dear ones?

We believe that G. Bush is not only playing with the life and destiny of the oppressed people of Afghanistan but is also bent upon ruining the future of the American generations. He seems to be fond of getting the title of "The Conqueror of the World". It is for this reason that he is following in the footsteps of [former German chancellor Adolf] Hitler and [former Russian president Leonid] Brezhnev, pursuing their hegemonic policies all over the world. But you must realize that history may repeat itself with America facing a similar

> *"Is it possible for a nation whose 25000 defenseless citizens have been brutally murdered to welcome the murderers of their sons?"*

catastrophic end as the Germans and Russians faced at the hands of Hitler and Brezhnev. If Bush and his allies are unable to conquer Afghanistan, how can they conquer the whole world? In the first six months of the war, your army dropped 72000 bombs and rockets, killed more than 25000 Afghans, spending more than 17 billion dollars but what it achieved must serve as an eye-opener for the same voices of America. The following is a bird's eye-view of your achievements:

a. The Taliban were removed from power and instead the pro-Russian Northern Alliance was imposed on the Afghan people, accomplishing a job which the Russians and their regional allies were unable to carry out despite their burning desires. Therefore, the real conqueror of Kabul is [Russian president Vladimir] Putin and not Bush. Today, Afghanistan is in the hands of pro-Russian groups and not under the rule of Americans. The Americans have no Afghan group on their side which is capable of ruling over Afghanistan. The sooner the Americans realize that the gangs gathered from Kabar and Nabel [in Kyrgyzstan in central Asia] cannot rule over a country like Afghanistan the better for them.

By invading Afghanistan, USA has served the interests of the following countries in the region:

1. Those which felt threatened by the regime of Taliban and supported the Northern Alliance with cash and weapons to get rid of Taliban.
2. Those which are ready for this kind of cooperation with the USA in any part of the world.
3. Those who claim that had it not been for their support and active contribution of Northern Alliance the Americans could never dislodge the Taliban with such case and celerity.

American Misjudgments

b. The Americans have apprehended some 600 people from Afghanistan and shifted them to the American base in Guantanamo. I am sure that even ten percent of these detainees are not important members of Taliban or al-Qaeda. The Americans must know that they will fail to crush such movements through their suppressive but failed policies. Those with even a little knowledge about such movements know that they are product of certain political conditions and can survive the shock of the arrest and elimination of their second and third tier leaders.

c. On insistence of Britain, the Americans brought to Afghanistan the aged and ailing ex-king, by the dent of sheer force and with an air of arrogance, to impose him on the people of Afghanistan in a bid to bolster the down-spiraling morale of the British monarchy and prove wrong those critics who say that the days of the outdated monarchies are numbered. These Americans knew little that this man was neither popular in Afghanistan nor capable of ruling and therefore they failed to crown him as the king of Afghanistan. They were never tired of trying to convince the world that [the ex-king] Zahir Khan is a popular figure in Afghanistan and that as such he is the only uncontroversial person who can united all ethnic groups of Afghanistan. The outcome of the American sponsored Loya Jirga [people's assembly] whose members were not elected by Afghan but were handpicked by Americans and their cronies should have proven for the Americans that Zahir Khan is the most controversial person in Afghanistan and that the nation may rally behind any personality except him. Sensing the danger and realizing the hatred of Afghans for this man, [Afghan foreign minister Zalmay] Khalilzad blocked the candidacy of Zahir Khan at the eleventh hour as he knew that his candidacy will result in a humiliating defeat for the Americans. This way the American drama to install the ex-king who had announced his candidature a day before the Loya Jirga in Kabul came to end. All those who voted for [president Hamid] Karzai cast their votes in his favour only to block the way of Zahir Khan.

U.S.-Imposed Puppets Rule Afghanistan

d. Boasting of the American achievements in Afghanistan, G. Bush brazenly tells the world that the Afghan ambassador in America is an American citizen; that Zalmay Khalilzad, a member of the national security council is his envoy in Afghanistan, that Hamid Karzai a onetime employee of an American oil company is the president of Afghanistan. Let me tell your president that such statements were issued once by Breshnev also. At that time when the Russian considered themselves, just the way the Americans imagine today, the masters of Afghan skies and lands, many official members of KGB [Russian Intelligence Organization] were considered rulers of Afghanistan. Mr. Bush should feel ashamed of stooping so low and bluffing and boasting in this manner and not take pride in it. Is it not a shameful act to invade sovereign states and impose your spies and employees on them? Or the rules of the international game have been changed for the Americans as is evident from the recent Bush doctrine? Mr. Bush should realize that only he and those as naïve as himself can believe that such puppets, who were not only imposed by Americans through sheer force but need also constant presence of their masters even for their personal security, are the real rulers of Afghanistan. How can a sane person consider such a puppet, 'welcomed' with bullets shot at his head when he goes to his hometown under the protection of the American troops, as the legitimate and real ruler of Afghanistan? If the Americans have failed during one whole year to guarantee their own security and that of their imposed puppets in Afghanistan as they constantly come under fire, their patrols are ambushed and their puppets presidents and ministers are attacked and killed, is it not enough for Mr. Bush and his friends to realize their mistake in Afghanistan and therefore revise their policy.

> *"Is it not a shameful act to invade sovereign states and impose your spies and employees on them?"*

U.S. Lies About American Casualties

e. The Americans also pursue a policy of disinformation and false propaganda with regard to the war in Afghanistan trying to keep the American nation in dark about the ground realities in Afghanistan. About the systematic rocket attacks on their bases, blamed by the Americans on the remnants of Taliban and al-Qaeda, they always claim that the rockets fell hundreds of meters away from the bases and thus did not entail any casualties. In some cases they admit that one or two soldiers were slightly wounded who later returned to active duty after treatment. The Afghans scornfully dismiss this disinformation as they know that the new aggressors are treading the path of their fellow Russians in hiding the real number of their casualty bags. The Americans are so brazenly lying about their casualties that they have left the Russians far behind. The number of dead Russian soldiers was announced when the Russians were booted out of Afghanistan and the Afghans are waiting to hear the real figure of the American casualties when they are also kicked out of Afghanistan or when a rival president is installed in the White House. Afghans are of the opinion that it is likely that the special forces of USA are mainly comprised of illegitimate children who have no parents and dependents to pressure the government to know their whereabouts and as such the government does not feel the need to announce their death. Otherwise, these Afghans say, we daily see their damaged vehicles, their spilled blood, their wounded and dead. Their patrols are ambushed routinely; their bases come under almost daily attacks and after every attack we see that the spot is cordoned and air surveillance and protection is provided immediately. Helicopters reach the scene and lift the casualties but the Americans prefer to remain tight-lipped about such attacks.

More American Deaths by Afghan Resistance

f. The fact of the matter is that these attacks on the American forces have intensified. . . . They are not organized by Taliban nor by al-Qaeda but they are revengeful acts carried out by those Afghans who have lost their dear and near ones in the barbaric bombardments by Americans, or their houses have been destroyed and their villages and mosques have been razed to the ground; their homes have been searched and they have been humiliated; their personal weapons have been confiscated. These are those Afghans who fought against the Russians for those same reasons but the ferocity and scope of

"These attacks [by the Afghan resistance] on the American forces have intensified."

the resistance as well as the number of enemy's casualties are much greater than they were in the resistance against the Russians in the first three months of their presence in Afghanistan. Presently, the average American casualty on the Afghan soil is more than one in five people with the graph shooting up almost vertically. The American casualties in each province of Kunar, Khost, and Kandahar are almost double the numbers of their casualties in the war of Kuwait. In the last three months, in each of these three provinces, more than forty Americans soldiers have lost their lives. Similarly, in Paktia and Paktika provinces, the number of casualties is on constant increase and soon the resistance would engulf other provinces also. You would better know that the slackness of resistance in other provinces is due to absences or very small numbers of American forces in those provinces and not because the people of those areas are less freedom-loving or have lost their sensitivity against occupation forces.

American Occupation Mirrors Russian Occupation

g. You should ask the Bush regime that on what grounds and for which political gains he has deployed American forces against Pakhtoons who constitute 65% of the Afghan people and why he is collaborating with minorities which were at the disposal of the regional alliance under the leadership of the Russians. Why is all the fighting staged in the areas of Pakhtoons and why are your forces engaged in fighting in these areas? Taliban ruled over a vast area of the north and they had supporters and followers there also. Why aren't your forces stationed in the north of Afghanistan? Nor are they engaged in battles there. They are not searching houses in the north, nor are they collecting weapons. Why are you dispatching Northern Alliance troops to the East and South, Pakhtoon areas, to fight against the people, search the houses and collect weapons and in the process humiliate the people? Why are you depending on those communist generals whose hands are still red with the blood of the innocent Afghans? Why is the pro-Russian alliance at your disposal today as it was serving its Russian master yesterday? Why are you fighting those whom the Russians were also fighting? The answer is quite clear: Those who do not bow down and surrender before the aggressor are the greatest culprits in your opinion as they were in the eyes of the Russian aggressors. But rest assured that they also will deal with you in a similar fashion as they dealt with the Russian.

> *"Rest assured . . . [the Afghan resistance] will deal with you in a similar fashion as they dealt with the [Russians]."*

h. When the Afghans hear from BBC or VoA [Voice of America] that after the American invasion of Afghanistan the first steps towards democracy have been taken (people freely listen to music, Indian films are on display in the cinema houses, video-cassette shops are on the increase, the laws on growing beards and wearing veils by the women have been repealed) they are astonished to find that your democracy and slogans are so identical with those of the first communist regime installed by the Russians. After their naked military aggression, they also claimed to have installed a democratic government to fight imperialism and reactionary forces. They also made the women depart with their veils; worked tirelessly to make music popular; opened nightclubs and casinos, adherence to Islamic rites and practices were considered the biggest crimes punishable by death and imprisonment; all the clergymen and practising Muslims were labeled as enemies of the revolution. Your are following in their footsteps with astonishing accuracy. The moment your soldiers attack any village the first bomb is dropped on the mosque and the first man apprehended is the village clergyman. Every Mujahid and Muslim is in your wanted list. The savageness of the American forces is reminiscent of the barbaric acts of the Russian troops. You are turning villages into graveyards as they did; massacres of captives in Qale Jangi (700), Kunduz and Shiberghan [Taliban strongholds in northern Afghanistan] where thousands were buried in mass graves have been committed under the orders of your generals and with active participation of your forces. The Afghans curse such 'democracy' which is no different from the Russian democracy. They despise this democracy of yours which means installation of foreign spies, puppets, war criminals and thieves through the barrel of gun and reviving the dreaded KHAD [Afghan secret police] which is responsible for the death of hundreds of thousands of innocent Afghans so that it can start its bloody game once again.

American Destruction of Afghanistan

i. The Americans even destroyed those facilities and national assets of Afghanistan which had escaped damage during the 23 years of war in that country. An example is the aeroplanes of the national airlines, Aryana, which were destroyed due to the American bombardment of all Afghan airports. The Americans did nothing to compensate for the great loss. Even they could not do what the Indians, out of rivalry with Pakistan, did—to give an old passenger airplane to Aryana. The Americans who have spent billions of dollars for destruction of Afghanistan and are ready to commit more money for more destruction could not spare a few million dollars to compensate for their crimes. No same person can understand this arrogant American attitude. People ask that why the Americans are testing their strength with the helpless Afghans. Why are they exploiting their economic and military strength and wishes? Instead of arrogance, insanity and such highhandedness, they should have taken pity on the oppressed nations of the world.

No Security and Opium Cultivation Booms

j. The Taliban government could establish such peace and security in the highways and the areas under their control which was consistently appreciated by you. The VoA used to say that the security established during the rule of Taliban was unique in the history of Afghanistan. They were able to ban poppy cultivation in all the areas under their control with a single ordinance. But you and your puppet interim administration have miserably failed to establish even a semblance of security or stop the new poppy cultivation craze. Today the Afghan highways are not safe; nor are the cities and areas under the control of the interim administration or the regional warlords safe and secure. Leave the plight of the common oppressed Afghans who are massacred, humiliated and dishonoured at the whims of the 'champion of democracy' in the world aside. Even the staff of the UN offices are not safe due to the excesses of the criminal warlords imposed on our nation by the Americans. The statement of [UN Special envoy to Afghanistan] Lakhdar Brahimi [concerning the murders of aid workers by U.S.-backed warlords] should have caused great embarrassment for the Americans had they any sense of sanity and morality. A female foreign staff member of UN was subjected to repeated gang rapes at the hands of your closest allies in

> *"How can those who destroy the peace and security of other peoples think that they will be spared?"*

the north, whom you proudly trust and brazenly support because they committed the worst kind of genocide in Qalae Jangi and Shiberghan where the mass graves speak volumes about the ethnic cleansing in Afghanistan at the whim of the Americans. Poppy cultivation in Afghanistan has witnessed an unprecedented boom under the interim government. The compensation money for the farmers whose poppy fields were destroyed was pocketed by your corrupt allies who used to destroy those fields whose opium had already been harvested more than once.

America Is Caught in Russia's Trap

k. Mr. Bush dragged the neighbouring countries of Afghanistan in his unjust war against our nation, sowing the seeds of permanent hostilities in the region and creating unsolvable internal problems. Those who claim to be qualified for the leadership of the world must justify their claims through their actions. True world leaders do not create tensions in the world nor do they work for escalation of hostilities. Instead they utilize their influence in de-escalation and reconciliation. On the other hand those who push the world to war or add fuel to the existing flames should not think that their own backyard would not remain safe. How can those who destroy the peace and and security of other peoples think that they will be spared and their own peace will not be disturbed? . . . It is beyond any shadow of doubt that your presence in Afghanistan will ensure the same catastrophic consequences which forced the Russians to leave Afghanistan in humiliation. Moscow, in our view, by supporting the American invasion of Afghanistan and directing its puppets in the Northern Alliance to fight against the oppressed nation under your command, has placed the most dangerous trap for the Americans to avenge their humiliating defeat in Afghanistan.

America's Failure in Afghanistan

l. With his threats of war against Iraq, Mr. Bush wants to make the world believe that his war against Afghanistan was a resounding victory which could be repeated elsewhere. He is also pretending that his concerns about the security of coming generations of America are prompting him to attack Iraq. But the truth of the matter is that the American invasion of Afghanistan has been a disastrous failure. The Americans have miserably failed to achieve their stated goals; they have failed to apprehend the leaders of Taliban and al-Qaeda; their wheeling and dealing for installing a government of their choice capable of serving their interests has yielded no tangible results. Neither they have been able to put an end to the ongoing fighting nor could they establish peace and security of their choice. The only tangible achievement of Bush administration from this war is the dead bodies of American youth and deep hatred of the Afghans for them.

m. If Mr. Bush is really concerned about the future of the Americans he should have been sincere and straightforward with them, confessing that his real aim of invading Iraq is to occupy the second largest oil reserves of the world, and not the much trumpeted aim of defending the Americans against imaginary threats from the atomic or chemical weapons that he perceives Iraq to be developing and may use one day against America. The world has a right to ask that how is it that the Americans have no fears and concerns about the established nuclear, biological and chemical weapons of Russia, China and Israel which could really threaten their peace, but suffer from such a great phobia about an impoverished, war-affected and sanction-ridden country like Iraq which does not have the required financial resources and technical expertise to develop such weapons. How can a country unable to defend its soil against the constant American aerial attacks develop such advanced weapons?

In our opinion, no wise and well-informed person could consider the American invasion of Afghanistan a success to be repeated at any other place in the world.

Further Involvement in Afghanistan Threatens America's Security

by Ron Paul

About the author: *Ron Paul represents the fourteenth congressional district of Texas in the U.S. House of Representatives.*

I rise in opposition to [the 2002 Freedom Support bill to support Afghanistan's reconstruction].[1] The President [George W. Bush] has not asked for this piece of legislation; he does not support it. We do not anticipate that it will be passed in the other body [the U.S. Senate]. But there is one good part of the bill, and that is the title, "Freedom Support." We all support freedom. It is just that this bill does not support freedom. Really, it undermines the liberties and the taxes of many Americans in order to pump another $1.2 billion into Afghanistan.

One of the moral justifications, maybe, for rebuilding Afghanistan is that it was the American bombs that helped to destroy Afghanistan in our routing of the Taliban [Islamic fundamentalist regime]. But there are a lot of shortcomings in this method. Nation-building does not work. I think this will fail. I do not think it will help us.

Social Engineering Will Fail

I do not think for a minute that this is much different than social engineering that we try here in the U.S. with a lot of duress and a lot of problems; and now we are going to do it over there where we really do not understand the social conditions that exist, and it is not like here. Some, especially those in that part of the world, will see this as neo-colonialism because we are over there for a lot of different reasons. And even in the bill it states one of the reasons. It says, "We are to design an overall strategy to advance U.S. interests in Afghanistan."

1. The Senate and House passed amended versions of the bill in 2003.

Ron Paul, address to the U.S. House Foreign Affairs Committee, Washington, DC, May 24, 2002.

Well, I wonder what that means? Over 10 years ago there was an explicit desire and a statement made by the administration that until we had a unified government in Afghanistan, we could not build a gas pipeline across northern Afghanistan. And that is in our interests. Does that mean this is one of the motivations?

I imagine a lot of people here in the Congress might say no, but that might be the ultimate outcome. It is said that this bill may cut down on the drug trade. But the Taliban was stronger against drugs than the Northern Alliance. Drug production is up since we've been involved this past year in Afghanistan. . . .

I think it is important to state first off that while it is true that the administration has not actively opposed this legislation, it certainly has not asked for nor does it support the Afghanistan Freedom Support Act. It did not support the bill when we marked it up in the International Relations Committee, it did not support the bill after it was amended in Committee, and it does not support the bill today. . . .

This Is Neo-Colonialism

Perhaps the "Afghanistan Freedom Support Act" should more accurately be renamed the "Afghanistan Territorial Expansion Act," because this legislation essentially treats that troubled nation like a new American territory. In fact, I wonder whether we give Guam, Puerto Rico, or other American territories anywhere near $1.2 billion every few years—so maybe we just should consider full statehood for Afghanistan. This new State of Afghanistan even comes complete with an American governor, which the bill charitably calls a "coordinator." After all, we can't just give away such a huge sum without installing an American overseer to ensure we approve of all aspects of the fledgling Afghan government. . . .

When we fill a nation's empty treasury, when we fund and train its military, when we arm it with our weapons, when we try to impose foreign standards and values within it, indeed when we attempt to impose a government and civil society of our own making upon it, we are nation-building. There is no other term for it. Whether Congress wants to recognize it or not, this is neo-colonialism. Afghanistan will be unable to sustain itself economically for a very long time to come, and during that time American taxpayers will pay the bills. This sad reality was inevitable from the moment we decided to invade it and replace its government, rather than use covert forces to eliminate the individuals truly responsible for [the September 11, 2001, terrorist attacks]. Perhaps

> *"Nation-building does not work. I think this will fail. I do not think it will help us."*

the saddest truth is that [terrorist mastermind Osama] Bin Laden remains alive and free even as we begin to sweep up the rubble from our bombs.

I am sure that supporters of this bill are well-intentioned, but judging from past experience this approach will fail to improve the lives of the average Afghan citizen. Though many will also attempt to claim that this bill is somehow about the attacks of 9/11, let's not fool ourselves: nation-building and social engineering are what this bill is about. Most of the problems it seeks to address predate the 9/11 attacks and those it purports to assist had nothing to do with those attacks.

If we are operating under the premise that global poverty itself poses a national security threat to the United States, then I am afraid we have an impossible task ahead of us.

As is often the case, much of the money authorized by this bill will go toward lucrative contracts with well-connected private firms and individuals. In short, when you look past all the talk about building civil society in Afghanistan and defending against terrorism, this bill is laden with the usual corporate welfare and hand-outs to special interests.

> *"Whether Congress wants to recognize it or not, this is neo-colonialism."*

The Drug War Is a Failure

Among other harmful things, this legislation dramatically expands the drug war. Under the group we have installed in Afghanistan, opium production has skyrocketed. Now we are expected to go in and clean up the mess our allies have created. In addition, this bill will send some $60 million to the United Nations, to help fund its own drug eradication program. I am sure most Americans agree that we already send the United Nations too much of our tax money, yet this bill commits us to sending even more.

The drug war has been a failure. Plan Colombia, an enormously expensive attempt to reduce drug production in that Andean nation, has actually resulted in a 25 percent increase in coca leaf and cocaine production. Does anyone still think our war on drugs there has been successful? Is it responsible to continue spending money on policies that do not work?

The bill also reflects a disturbing effort by the Washington elite to conduct experiments in social engineering in Afghanistan. It demands at least five times that the Afghans create a government that is "broad-based, multi-ethnic, gender-sensitive, and fully representative." We are imposing race and gender quotas on a foreign government that have been found inappropriate and in some cases even illegal in the United States. Is this an appropriate activity to be carried out with taxpayer funds? . . .

The problem with nation-building and social-engineering, as experience tells us time and time again is that it simply doesn't work. We cannot build multi-ethnic, multi-cultural, gender-sensitive civil society and good governance in Afghanistan on a top-down basis from afar. What this bill represents is a commitment to deepening involvement in Afghanistan and a determination to impose a political system on that country based on a blueprint drawn up thousands of miles away by Washington elites. Does anyone actually believe that we can buy Afghan democracy with even the staggering sum of 1.2 billion dollars? A real democracy is the product of shared values and the willingness of a population to demand and support it. None of these things can be purchased by a foreign power. What is needed in Afghanistan is not just democracy, but freedom—the two are not the same.

No Way to Teach Democracy

Release of funds authorized by this legislation is dependent on the holding of a traditional Afghan assembly of tribal representatives—a "loya jirga"—as a first step toward democratization. It authorizes $10 million to finance this meeting. That this traditional meeting will produce anything like a truly representative body is already in question, as we heard earlier this month [May 2002] that seven out of 33 influential tribal leaders have already announced they will boycott the meeting. Additionally, press reports have indicated that the U.S. government itself was not too long ago involved in an attempted assassination of a non-Taliban regional leader who happened to be opposed to the rule of the American-installed Hamid Karzai. More likely, this "loya jirga" will be a stage-managed showpiece, primarily convened to please Western donors. Is this any way to teach democracy? . . .

Some two decades ago the Soviet Union also invaded Afghanistan and attempted to impose upon the Afghan people a foreign political system. Some nine years and 15,000 Soviet lives later they retreated in disgrace, morally and financially bankrupt. During that time, we propped up the Afghan resistance with our weapons, money, and training, planting the seeds of the Taliban in the process. Now the former Soviet Union is gone, its armies long withdrawn from Afghanistan, and we're left cleaning up the mess—yet we won't be loved for it. No, we won't get respect or allegiance from the Afghans, especially now that our bombs have rained down upon them. We will pay the bills, however Afghanistan will become a tragic ward of the American state, another example of an interventionist foreign policy that is supposed to serve our national interests and gain allies, yet which does neither.

I repeat that the President has not been interested in this legislation. I do not see a good reason to give him the burden of reporting back to us in 45 days to explain how he is going to provide for Afghan security for the long term. How long is long term? We have been in Korea now for 50 years. Are we planning to send troops that provide national security for Afghanistan? I think we should be more concerned about the security of this country and not wondering how we are going to provide the troops for long-term security in Afghanistan. We should be more concerned about the security of our ports. . . .

Harmful to America's Poor

Over the last several days and almost continuously, as a matter of fact, many Members get up and talk about any expenditure or any tax cut as an attack on Social Security, but we do not hear this today because there is a coalition, well built, to support this intervention and presumed occupation of Afghanistan. But the truth is, there are monetary and budget consequences for this.

After this bill is passed, if this bill is to pass, we will be close to $2 billion in aid to Afghanistan, not counting the military. Now, that is an astounding amount of money, but it seems like it is irrelevant here. Twelve months ago, the national debt was $365 billion less than it is today, and people say we are just getting away from having surpluses. Well, $365 billion is a huge deficit, and the national debt is going up at that rate. April revenues were down 30 percent from 1 year ago. The only way we pay for programs like this is either we rob Social Security or we print the money, but both are very harmful to poor people and people living on a limited income. Our funds are not unlimited. I know there is a lot of good intention; nobody in this body is saying we are going over there to cause mischief, but let me tell my colleagues, there is a lot of reasons not to be all that optimistic about these wonderful results and what we are going to accomplish over there. . . .

Earlier the gentleman from California ([congressman in the U.S. House of Representatives] Mr. Rohrabacher) came up with an astounding reason for us to do this. He said that we owe this to Afghanistan. Now, I have heard all kinds of arguments for foreign aid and foreign intervention, but the fact that we owe this to Afghanistan? Do we know what we owe? We owe responsibility to the American taxpayer. We owe responsibility to the security of this country.

> *"Afghanistan will become . . . another example of an interventionist foreign policy that is supposed to serve our national interests and gain allies, yet which does neither."*

One provision of this bill takes a $300 million line of credit from our DOD [Department of Defense] and just gives the President the authority to take $300 million of weapons away from us and give it to somebody in Afghanistan. Well, that dilutes our defense, that does not help our defense. This is not beneficial. We do not need to have an occupation of Afghanistan for security of this country. There is no evidence for that.

The occupation of Afghanistan is unnecessary. It is going to be very costly, and it is very dangerous. My colleagues might say, well, this is all for democracy. For democracy? Well, did we care about democracy in Venezuela? It seemed like we tried to undermine that just recently. Do we care about the democracy in Pakistan? A military dictator takes over and he becomes our best ally, and we use his land, and yet he has been a friend to the Taliban, and who knows, bin Laden may even be in Pakistan. Here we are saying we are doing it all for democracy. Now, that is just pulling our leg a little bit too much. This is not the reason that we are over there. We are over there for a lot of other reasons and, hopefully, things will be improved.

U.S. Efforts Will Fail

But I am terribly concerned that we will spend a lot of money, we will become deeply mired in Afghanistan, and we will not do a lot better than the Soviets did. Now, that is a real possibility that we should not ignore. We say, oh, no, everything sounds rosy and we are going to do this, we are going to do it differently, and this time it is going to be okay. Well, if we look at the history of that land and that country, I would think that we should have second thoughts.

It has been said that one of the reasons why we need this legislation is to help pay for drug eradication. Now, that is a good idea. That would be nice if we could do that. But the drug production has exploded since we have been there. In the last year, it is just going wild. Well, that is even more reason we have to spend money because we contributed to the explosion of the drug production. There is money in this bill, and maybe some good will come of this; there is money in this bill that is going to be used to teach the Afghan citizens not to use drugs. . . .

If this is successful, if we teach the Afghan people not to use drugs, that would be wonderful. Maybe then we can do something about the ravenous appetite of our people for drugs which is the basic cause of so much drug production.

So to spend money on these kinds of programs I think is just a little bit of a stretch. Already there have been 33 tribal leaders that have said they will not attend this Loya Jirga, that they are not going to attend. The fact that we are going to spend millions of dollars trying to gather these people together and tell them what to do with their country, I think the odds of producing a secure country are slim.

Already in the papers just a few weeks ago it was reported in *The Washington Post* that our CIA made an attempt to assassinate a former prime minister of Afghanistan. He may have been a bum for all I know, but do Members [of the U.S. House of Representatives] think that sits well? He was not an ally of bin Laden, he was not a Taliban member, yet our CIA is over there getting involved. As a matter of fact, that is against our law, if that report is true. Yet, that is what the papers have reported.

A Dangerous Predicament

So I would say that we should move cautiously. I think this is very dangerous. I know nobody else has spoken out against this bill, but I do not see much benefit coming from this. I know it is well motivated, but it is going to cost a lot of money, we are going to get further engaged, more troops are going to go over there; and now that we are a close ally of Pakistan, we do know that Pakistan and India both have nuclear weapons, and we are sitting right next to them. So I would hardly think this is advantageous for our security, nor advantageous for the American people, nor advantageous to the American taxpayer.

I see this as a threat to our security. It does not reassure me one bit. This is what scares me. It scares me when we send troops into places like Vietnam and Korea and other places, because it ultimately comes back to haunt us.

Chapter 4

What Form of Government Is Best for Afghanistan?

Chapter Preface

For almost three decades Afghanistan's efforts to establish a strong stable government based on the values of the Afghan people has been undermined by other countries. For example, in the 1970s and 1980s, the Soviet Union and the United States vied for control on Afghanistan's soil during the Cold War. "Over the past thirty years, Afghanistan has been a showcase for global confrontation," said Afghan president Hamid Karzai. "Transnational phenomena came to clash with each other. . . . Neither communism nor extremism, nor terrorism were homegrown in Afghanistan."

In order to determine the Afghan people's vision for their nation, representatives of the international community met with Afghan leaders in Bonn, Germany, in December 2001 following the defeat of the ruling Taliban regime by U.S.-led forces. The participants at the Bonn conference appointed an interim administration under Karzai's leadership to guide the country until a national election was held in which the Afghan people could decide who would lead their nation on the road to peace, prosperity, and stability.

Although all parties acknowledged that the plans made at the Bonn conference were a step in the right direction, they also granted that the success of these plans depended on other countries respecting the sovereignty of the Afghan people. To formalize their commitment to refrain from destructive interference in Afghan affairs, in a historic meeting in December 2002, Afghanistan and its neighbors—China, Iran, Pakistan, Tajikistan, Turkmenistan, and Uzbekistan—signed the Kabul Declaration. In the declaration the signatories agreed to honor "the principles of territorial integrity, mutual respect, friendly relations, cooperation, and non-interference in each other's internal affairs."

Although commentators agree that the establishment of a stable government in Afghanistan depends on other countries not interfering in Afghan affairs, they disagree on the likelihood of other nations' restraint. According to Hooman Peimani, author of *Falling Terrorism and Rising Conflicts: The Afghan Contribution to Polarization and Confrontation in West and South Asia*, the conditions that caused the competition among external actors that led to wars in Afghanistan have not changed. For example, the United States, Russia, and China still want to protect their oil interests in central Asia. Because Afghanistan's neighbors still have a vested interest in the nation's affairs, Peimani concludes that attempts to establish a stable Afghan government will probably fail, resulting in civil war.

Karzai, on the other hand, believes that the world changed after the September 11, 2001, terrorist attacks on the United States. He says world leaders now acknowledge the interdependence of all human beings and have a new spirit of cooperation. "Never was the world . . . more united than in the aftermath of 11

September 2001. . . . Afghanistan is demonstrating that the cooperation [rather than the clash] of civilizations is possible." Although many commentators do not agree with Karzai's assessment, they do concur that stability and peace in Afghanistan depends on world leaders making Karzai's vision the prevailing global reality for the twenty-first century. In the following chapter authors give their views on the preferred form of government for Afghanistan.

The U.S. Presidential Model of Democracy Is Best for Afghanistan

by Hamid Karzai

About the author: Hamid Karzai is the president of Afghanistan. During the Soviet occupation from 1979 to 1989 Karzai was active in the Afghan resistance, and in 1992, he became Afghanistan's foreign minister. After the fall of the Taliban regime, he was appointed head of the Interim Administration of Afghanistan until he was elected president by Afghanistan's Loya Jirga *(people's assembly) in June 2002. On October 9, 2004, Karzai was elected president in the country's first general election.*

Allow me to take a few minutes to tell you why, as an individual member of the Afghan nation, and as the President of this country, I have expressed my preference for a presidential system of government, while a parliamentary system, as an alternative, can also be said to serve the interest of democracy and people's choices. But let me first say a few words about each of the two systems of government.

In a parliamentary system, people from all over the country elect delegates from among election contenders who are either fielded by different political parties, or stand as independent candidates. After elected candidates come to the parliament, the party with most seats form the government, and governments can enjoy both stability and continuity. The president in this system is a symbolic figurehead, appointed by the parliament, and does not interfere in government. The prime minister is the chief executive, and he can, if he thinks it is necessary, dissolve the parliament and go towards fresh elections.

Where any single party fails to obtain enough seats to form the government, two or more small parties or groups sit together, creating a coalition which then forms the government. I believe such a situation would be quite dangerous for Afghanistan in the present context where strong state institutions are absent. It bodes in-

Hamid Karzai, address to the Closing Session of the *Loya Jirga*, Afghanistan, January 2004.

stability. This basically was the reason that I advocated for a presidential system.

So what are the demands of a presidential system? In a presidential system the president is elected by the whole nation, through direct vote by the people. The people also elect the parliament through direct vote. So there is a president, and there is a parliament, one in charge of the executive power, and the other of the legislative power; with a judiciary that is independent.

In the presidential system we have now adopted in the constitution, the president cannot dissolve the parliament. As long as there is the president, there is the parliament. If the president commits an erroneous act, the parliament alerts him or her to the error, and this helps the country to be stable, and the government to be sustainable. This is why I thought this was the best option. But it has other advantages too.

Presidential Versus Parliamentary System

Of course the constitution is a document that can be amended. The constitution shall be respected. Its implementation is essential, and requires strong determination by the nation. But the constitution is not [the Islamic holy book] the Quran. If five or ten years down the line we find that stability improves, proper political parties emerge, and we judge that a parliamentary system can function better, then a Loya Jirga [people's assembly] can at a time of our choosing be convened to adopt a different system of government.

The other aim behind opting for a presidential system at present was the fear that, under a parliamentary system, the country may be divided among political parties which are formed along ethnic lines, or split into small parties, which are disposed to forming alliances and coalition along ethnic, sectarian or regional lines in order to be able to govern. This would limit the possibility of the emergence of national, inclusive political parties.

In Britain, which is perhaps the most stable parliamentary system in the world, they have a queen who does not interfere in government, and a parliament which elects a prime minister from its midst. They have two strong parties, the Conservative Party and the Labour Party, either of which is capable of winning an election and forming a government that is stable throughout the five years of the parliamentary period.

In India, for as long as the Congress Party enjoyed an absolute majority support, they used to have stable governments. As the Congress gradually declined, and other parties rose to

> *"I believe . . . [the parliamentary system] would be quite dangerous for Afghanistan in the present context where strong state institutions are absent."*

challenge it, India was delivered to coalition governments, each collapsing after another before completing even one year in office. Italy, in the aftermath of the Second World War, until a few years ago, saw more than 45 governments.

Thus, we thought that a presidential system was a better choice for Afghanistan in its present circumstances.

National, Not Ethnic, Allegiance

Dear brothers and sisters, my vision for the future of Afghanistan is of a country with big political parties, where anyone aspiring to become the president will depend on all the people of Afghanistan, and strive to build an inclusive political party as a platform. A platform in which any individual, from whichever corner of the country he may happen to originate, can ascend to the top of the ladder. My vision is that in Afghanistan anyone aspiring to achieve the post of president will depend on his own persuasion, capacity and competence, and the backing of a national and inclusive political party, not on an ethnic group, a region, or affiliation with a minority or a majority. Our vision for Afghanistan is of a country where people relate to each other through reason and shared ideas, convictions and behaviour, not through ethnic bonds, because this is not the way of building nations.

We want an Afghanistan where each member of the nation, regardless of which corner of the country they come from, have equal rights and economic opportunities, and are able—should they choose to—to contend to become the president of the country.

> *"Anyone aspiring to achieve the post of president will depend on his own . . . capacity and competence . . . not on an ethnic group, a region, or affiliation."*

I never want, neither do you—I am sure—that a person who belongs to the majority ethnic group necessarily becomes the president, and another belonging to the second largest ethnic group becomes the vice president, leaving the leftovers to the smaller ethnic groups. I do not want such an Afghanistan.

I want an Afghanistan where a poor boy from Yakawlang [in northeast Afghanistan] may rise to claim the chair of the president. I want an Afghanistan where a poor Baluchi [originally an ethnic group from Baluchistan, province of Pakistan] from Nimroz [in southwest Afghanistan] may achieve the president's post. To speak more frankly, I do not want that the president will necessarily be expected to be a Pashtun [the dominant ethnic group of Afghanistan] the vice-president a Tajik [from northeast Afghanistan], with Hazara [central Afghanistan], Uzbek [northwest Afghanistan] and so on following the line. No, this is not the Afghanistan I aspire to build. And if you do, I disagree with you.

I want an Afghanistan where the son of Kunduz goes to Nangarhar to run for the president; and in fact wins there because of his capacity, his competence, and because he has the legitimate backing of a party that is truly national in character.

One day I said to the respected Ustad [master musician], Ustad [former president Mr Burhanuddin] Rabbani: "go to Kandahar [in southeast Afghanistan] and campaign for yourself, and defeat me there, and know that I will defeat you in Badakhshan".

This is my Afghanistan. And this is the kind of Afghanistan that I wish to attain. I want anyone who intends to be a candidate in the future to come forward with the goal of helping this country develop into a strong nation, a nation where citizens have equal rights and abide by the law.

> *"Today [the United States of] America is among the greatest countries of the planet. . . . Because . . . ethnic divisions . . . do not exist."*

I once told [vice president, Mr Karim] Khalili sahib that if he wants to succeed he should come out of Hazarajat [in central Afghanistan], and speak to the rest of Afghanistan. I told [Vice President Marshall Mohammad Qaseem] Fahim Khan to come out of Panjsher; don't sit there forever; go and show to the people of Afghanistan that you are better and more qualified than Karzai. Go and succeed, and defeat me.

This country needs political courage, not timidity, and certainly not political and ethnic conservatism.

U.S. Model

Today [the United States of] America is among the greatest countries of the planet. It provides help to all others in the world. Its helicopters often take us when we need to travel to inaugurate our roads. Why? Because America is a country where minorities and majorities do not exist, where ethnic divisions and interests do not exist. When you become American, then you are an American, full stop. You have rights, duties and obligations. In America, they have two major [political] parties there—the Republicans and the Democrats. They contend in elections, one becomes the president, the other gives consent. And they both sit in the parliament.

Brothers, do you follow me? That is the kind of Afghanistan I want, nothing less. One year ago [in 2003] on my visit to Kandahar, at the invitation of [the then Kandahar governor] Gul Agha Sherzai, I was staying overnight in the old Governor House where two to three hundred people were staying. As we got up to go for the evening prayers, an elderly man came up to me and introduced himself. He then said: "I want to tell you that you will belong to us, only if you belong to the whole of Afghanistan first. Otherwise, you don't belong to us."

On another visit to Kandahar, a few minutes before I became the target of the assassination attempt, as we came out of kherqa-i-mubarak (holy cloak) shrine, I stood by to greet the women and children who had gathered near the shrine. A boy, who was eight or nine years old, came up hopping around and I heard him say: "You're the leader of Afghanistan, welcome to Kandahar". He did not say you are a Kandahari, so welcome to Kandahar.

Dear brothers and sisters, We have to set our goals high. Once in Badakhshan, on the road between Faizabad and Baharak, we alighted by the Khwaja Abdal-i-Wali shrine. There was a small wooden shack where an elderly man sat selling tiny melons among other things. The seller gave me a melon which I found very delicious, having been famished. I said to him, "may God make your shop as big as Afghanistan". He replied: "Don't pray like that, Sir. Pray that may God make Afghanistan good, and I will be good too". I think this man was a real Afghan, because he saw his prosperity embedded in that of Afghanistan.

A Just Society

Dear representatives of the people, today you proved that you want an Afghanistan that is free of discrimination. This country has seen cruelty and injustice. Our past history is witness to injustice done to certain qawms (ethnic groups). Our recent history has seen a lot of injustice too. Foreigners have subjected our land to injustice. Invaders, with filthy collaborating hands from inside, have subjected this land to injustice. We have seen much, and we have grown more hard-bitten.

We, therefore, see our own interest, and the interest of Afghanistan, best served in a society, and through a system, that is free of discrimination. We need a society where everyone, from a student of the elementary grade to the person who is the head of state, stand equal before the law. We want a society based on law. Today, we created a constitution in order to bring about a law-abiding society.

But is it enough to have a constitution? Certainly not? As [Mr Lakhdar] Brahimi sahib said, a constitution can be no more than a stack of papers. There has to exist a national will (irrada-i-millee) to put principles into practice. And there has to exist a national administration (iddara-i-millee) to ensure the implementation of the law.

I was following the proceedings of the Loya Jirga carefully—don't assume I didn't know what was going on around here. I know there were debates. There were debates about Muqawamat (Resistance), and there were debates about languages. Sometimes these debates were quite heated, sometimes less so. This is the character of democracy. Parliaments in other parts of the world also debate. They even fight, and throw chairs at each other. So there is nothing to worry about conflicting views and about debates. We, in this Loya Jirga of ours, proved to the world that, despite the thirty years of trouble and misfortune, we continue to be a decent, cultured and articulate nation. The world has in fact acknowledged that Afghans do listen, and do respect the expression of free will. . . .

> "Sometimes . . . debates were quite heated, sometimes less so. This is the character of democracy."

Unprecedented Steps Toward Democracy

Our new constitution also takes a democratic step that is not only unprecedented in the history of Afghanistan, but of the region as a whole. You were able to agree to give official status to all minority languages in Afghanistan, in order to enable the speakers of those languages to study in their mother tongues. This is quite an innovative step that has precedence only in societies that are strong and solid. In Norway, which is perhaps one of the world's richest nations, even a language that is spoken by 20 or 30 thousand people in a village or town is an official language and people can learn to read it and write in it.

It is a proud a powerful step today that you recognised the language of your Uzbek brothers as official. I am confident, and you can be witness to this, that this step will inshallah [God willing] make Afghanistan a stronger and exemplary nation in the region. This step will further solidify the foundations of this nation and make us even prouder than we are.

I pray to God for a time when this nation will be able to speak to itself in all of its major languages. I have resolved to learn Uzbek language, and I will do it. I will tell them in their own language: "My fellow countrymen, I wish you well, congratulations to you!"

It is good to be able to speak the language of one's fellow countrymen. It is gratifying for me to be able to switch between Farsi [a Persian language] and Pashto [an Afghan language spoken by the majority of Afghans] so fluently. I will, if I can, learn Uzbek, Pashaee and Baluchi.

> *"We want an Afghanistan where government is accountable to people . . . and chosen through the direct expression of the people's will."*

Power in the world comes from unity and togetherness, not from disunity. And it demands courage. You had the courage and may God reward you for that. Afghanistan has two major official languages, Pashto and Dari, which we have proudly spoken for centuries. These two languages will be equally implemented as official medium in all state organizations. My office does this already. I speak and write in Dari, as I do in Pashto. Others will do the same.

Among the desires of the nation is the collection of weapons. For as long as there are weapons spread around, the nation will not enjoy security. This wish will be achieved.

We will remake the administration. We will get rid of corruption.

We will want an Afghanistan where no family suffers from hunger and poverty; an Afghanistan where every village and city will have roads, and electricity; an Afghanistan where women and elderly men are not forced to undertake arduous journeys to travel to a neighbouring country for treatment; an Afghanistan where people will not need to go abroad to find jobs, but where people from other countries will come to work; an Afghanistan that is governed by law, not guns and violence.

144

The Future Afghanistan

We want an Afghanistan where government is accountable to people; an Afghanistan where government is legitimate and chosen through the direct expression of the people's will. We want an Afghanistan whose flag is elevated in the world; an Afghanistan that has dignity and is respected by the outside world.

We want an Afghanistan where there is no injustice; an Afghanistan where laws can be implemented.

We want an Afghanistan whose children will not have to go abroad to get a decent education; where others can expect to come and be educated in a decent manner.

An Afghanistan whose treasury is respectable, and respected. This is the kind of Afghanistan that we want.

You have shown us today the way to such an Afghanistan. This constitution will be our guide. As a nation, we need to vow that we will follow the way.

Take this sincere promise from me that, for as long as I am here as the President, and until there are elections that bring a new president, I will be obedient to the law, and obedient to the national desires. I will not bend or swerve, and if I did, you will, I expect, show me the door.

If today you have laid the foundation for this Afghanistan, then you deserve my congratulations.

The U.S. Presidential Model of Democracy Will Fail in Afghanistan

by Peter van Onselen and Wayne Errington

About the authors: *Peter van Onselen is a lecturer on politics at Edith Cowan University in Perth, Western Australia, and Wayne Errington is a lecturer on politics at Charles Stuart University in Albany, New South Wales, Australia.*

With the attention of the world on the fate of [Iraqi leader] Saddam [Hussein], the people of Afghanistan are about to make a serious mistake. The country's *loya jirga* (constitutional assembly) is considering adopting a presidential model of democratisation along US lines. If it chooses such a system it will virtually guarantee the failure of its nascent democracy.

Incumbent Afghani president Hamid Karzai, supported by the United States, is seeking a strong executive presidency. His opponents naturally prefer that he should share power with a prime minister appointed by a constituent assembly. This type of argument has been played out endlessly over the past 30 years of democratic transitions.

Political scientists really don't know much. In fact, about the only thing we know for sure is that presidential systems don't work. There is only one example of a successful presidential democracy—the US. Unfortunately, the US happens to be in a unique position to impose or encourage the replication of its political institutions in other nations.

Where the US model has been exported, democracy has failed at its first try. Every time. In Latin America, which was strongly influenced by the American Revolution, presidential systems degenerated into military dictatorships. In our own [Asia-Pacific] region, dictatorial presidents took power away from legislatures in South Korea and the Philippines.

The problem is that the essence of American democracy lies not in its presidential executive, but in the separation of powers. It has proved very easy to transplant the former institution but nigh on impossible to develop the latter quickly enough to prevent the president from dominating the other branches of government. American colonies had long developed a tradition of independent courts and legislatures before independence.

Charismatic or ruthless leaders inevitably use the personal nature of the presidential office to argue the case for strong leadership to overcome the problems that face newly minted democracies. In Russia and Belarus, strong presidents have sidelined weak legislatures by claiming that party politics is corrupt, divisive and ineffectual.

Separation of Powers, Not Presidentialism

Even in the US, the presidency was envisaged as a much less dominant office than that we see today. Americans should export the separation of powers instead of presidentialism; building these competing institutions is a difficult but essential task for the consolidation of democracy.

The most successful US attempts to bring about democratic regimes have been in Germany and Japan—both parliamentary systems. The reason that British colonies have been so successful in building democracies after independence is the long tradition of independent courts and vigorous parliaments. But, as [African leader] Robert Mugabe has shown, determined leaders can overpower these institutions.

> *"Political scientists really don't know much. In fact, about the only thing we know for sure is that presidential systems don't work."*

No doubt, advisers to the Afghan government are counting on the urbane, self-effacing Karzai to behave himself as president. And he probably will, but what about his successor? Karzai warned the *loya jirga* that a parliamentary system would "become bogged down in political quarrels". One would hope so. That would be a tremendous alternative to the dispute resolution procedures of Afghanistan's recent past.

All executive governments complain about the hurdles they need to jump to enact legislation—the opposition, the courts, the people. Our own [former Australian prime minister] Paul Keating reflected on the "unrepresentative swill" that tends to populate democratic parliaments, while his successor [Australian prime minister John Howard], seeks to emasculate his parliamentary opposition through changes to the constitution.

Parliamentary System Is the Best Model

The most important thing for new democracies to learn is that elections are no panacea. Impatience with democratic methods invites frustrated voters to turn to a strong leader, but the record of such tyrants in solving their countries' problems is pretty dismal.

The model for Afghanistan should be neither the US system nor the British parliamentary type, with its myth of responsible government. Instead, the power-sharing parliamentary systems of "old Europe" provide the best model for new democracies. Fractured countries like Afghanistan and Iraq need to build national consensus through sharing power in cabinets and assemblies. The best way to bring this about is through a system of proportional representation.

A Democratic Nation-State May Not Be the Best Model for Afghanistan

by Matthew Riemer

About the author: *U.S.-based author Matthew Riemer—who writes on art, philosophy, religion, psychology, and politics—is the director of operations for* YellowTimes.org, *an alternative online news source that features unconventional viewpoints.*

Though the wars fought in Afghanistan and Iraq were tactically dissimilar and of varying levels of intensity, the post-war social, cultural, and political factors at play are very similar. The most relevant and foundational similarity between the two countries is their creation: each was cobbled together from amongst a plethora of local, autonomous/tribal regions into reluctant wholes in the form of what the conquering country felt to be a modern nation-state. And for both, since their involuntary birth, this fact has hampered their development, as well as posing a deep, historical puzzle for, first, Great Britain and, now, the United States, in their efforts at "nation building."

This predicament—if only in the name of thoroughness—must eventually elicit a series of important questions from the concerned observer, some of which might be:

- What are the inherent weaknesses of the "nation-state" model?
- When Washington uses the phrase "nation building," what does this really imply?
- Is the so-called "nation-state" a viable model for Afghanistan and Iraq?

Assessing the Nation-State Model

The United States may be uncovering a troublesome truth in its latest global endeavors: the fact that the nation-state is not a universal model for all regions and peoples of the world, and, in some cases, it may even obstruct the development of the very stability and select economic development the United States is seeking through its operations—especially in areas with a concentration of ethnic diversity like in the Balkans, the Caucasus, and much of Central Asia where state-sized regions more readily stabilize under a sub-network of autonomous zones defined by some obvious feature, whether it be ethnic, linguistic or geographical. The dominant US polity has always assumed that the keys to American success are the keys to global success, that what works for them will work for others. This belief has led many in the US leadership to think that concepts like democracy and free market capitalism can be smoothly exported to other regions and environments and have the same effect that they had in 18th and 19th century America. This widely held belief is shared by the Bush administration and has been explicitly stated in its 2002 National Security Strategy.

US Circumstances Contrast with Those of Afghanistan and Iraq

However, unlike modern day Afghanistan and Iraq, America, at the time of its founding, consisted of a single ruling class that came together to codify the social and economic rules that others would live by and best continue their prosperity. These individuals were all wealthy, Caucasian, Christian males who shared broad and overlapping interests. These so-called "founding fathers" also decided upon their inherent and inevitable sovereignty and its announcement at a time and place of their choosing.

> *"The nation-state . . . model . . . may even obstruct the development of the very stability and . . . economic development the United States is seeking through its operations."*

This picture, to even the most casual of observers, paints a perfect contrast with the countries the United States is currently attempting nation building in today. Both countries represent a diverse array of languages, religions and cultural traditions, while encompassing regions that were never unified in the sense that a modern day independent state is. This fact alone complicates the democratic process to the point of futility: the biggest obstacle being the interests of minority groups within any given state.

But this is a painful reality for Washington to accept as it greatly affects the continuation of economic paradigms so cherished throughout the centers of power in the Western world. If the Bush administration, other influential world leaders and future US administrations were to accept a greater amount of regional autonomy in distant lands—like by letting Iraq splinter into three independent states or at least autonomous regions—this would greatly affect the implementation of laws concerning free trade and deregulation; such political forms provide infrastructural barriers to the rather organic growth of free market economies. By being self-contained and, to a certain degree, self-reliant, regions where such a process were to take place inhibit the plans of Washington's economists.

US Interests at Risk

There are other concerns, however, when hypothetically imagining the break-up of larger states into multiple smaller ones. One of the biggest of these fears is the potential shift in regional power balances. For example, if southern Iraq were to become its own state completely dominated by Shi'ites, this would un-doubtedly portend some kind of union with Iran possibly to the point of annexation on the part of Tehran. If the Kurds in the north were to gain their independence this would ruffle Turkey and put diplomatic pressure on Washington. This is obviously not in the interests of the United States.

> *"[Afghanistan] represents a diverse array of languages, religions and cultural traditions. . . . This fact alone complicates the democratic process to the point of futility."*

Further east in Central Asia, reflections on Afghanistan produce similar results. Though Afghanistan is different from Iraq in that it has endured failed government after failed government for decades with regular periods of anarchy—warlords unconvincingly filling the power vacuums—while Iraq was ruled consistently by centralized power. If Afghanistan were to fragment it would be more difficult to predict what may happen—virtually all the warlords have both fought and been allied with one another at some point. Certainly the border between Afghanistan and Pakistan in the south and east would completely blur if the Pashtuns were to realize a long-awaited Pashtunistan; in the eyes of Washington, this would provide an undesirable strategic boost for Islamabad [Pakistan] despite their partnership in the US "war on terrorism." And, like in Iraq, Iran could be expected to curry favor with those along its border—Iranian border patrols did skirmish with the Taliban from time to time—such as the governor of Herat, Ismail Khan.

Because of such potential for unpredictable and dangerous events, such state fragmentation will remain a non-starter for Washington—market growth, acquisition and stability are just too at risk in that kind of environment.

Democracy May Invite Instability

So in this categorical rejection of new, or perhaps old, political forms, the United States must realize what that rejection brings to the table: the situation currently faced by the occupying forces in both Afghanistan and Iraq today. In both countries, diverse groups with less overlapping agendas than more are jockeying for position in a post-war context that features low-intensity guerrilla warfare, an occupying army, and the marginalization of large percentages of the population.

It remains a dubious proposition that both Afghanistan and Iraq can be shaped into fully functioning and integrated (within the globalized economic infra-structure) nation-states capable of long periods of stability, relative peace, and economic growth. The United States must decide what it really wants. Does it want democracy? And if it does, it must realize what democracy can actually mean in volatile regions such as Afghanistan and Iraq. Instability and democracy are not mutually exclusive conditions—democracy does not equal stability—and revolution—regardless of what one conceives it to be—is a democratic expression. Given a true choice, many people in many countries may feel no solidarity with a colonially created "nation."

Capitalism, Not Democracy, Is the Preferred System for Afghanistan

by Steven E. Landsburg

About the author: *Steven E. Landsburg is an associate professor of economics at the University of Rochester, New York.*

Do we try to nudge Afghanistan in the direction of democracy and civil liberties? To what end? India is a democracy with civil liberties, and it is mired in poverty. But Hong Kong, with no history of democratic institutions, is one of the wealthiest places on earth. If we want to bring Afghans into the modern world—the world of prosperity and technological advancement and economic growth, where one learns to appreciate cultural differences as opportunities for mutually beneficial trade—we should nudge them (insofar as we are capable of nudging) not toward democracy but toward capitalism. If you want to lift people out of starvation, political freedom is a luxury. Economic freedom is a necessity.

India and Hong Kong illustrate a general principle: There is not much relationship between political freedom and per capita income. That's not just a guess; it's based on numbers from Freedom House, a nonpartisan think tank and advocacy group that ranks political freedom in various countries on a scale from 1 to 7, based on criteria like free elections, significant opposition parties, and representation for cultural and ethnic minorities. Countries with the most political freedom (those rated 1) do have higher per capita incomes on average, but there are many exceptions. And below the top end, the connection becomes even more tenuous: There's very little difference in per capita income between countries rated 2 and countries rated 7.

By contrast, economic freedom—that is, limited government, functioning markets, well-enforced property rights, and an absence of barriers to international trade—really matters. Canada's Fraser Institute, in cooperation with 50 other economic think tanks around the world, ranks countries in terms of economic freedom, with Hong Kong at the head of the list, followed by Singapore, New Zealand, the United Kingdom and the United States. (The United States loses points for its widely varying tariff rates and restrictions on capital transactions with foreigners.) Algeria and Myanmar bring up the rear; Afghanistan, Iraq, and Saudi Arabia are unrated due to the unavailability of data, but presumably would have given Myanmar stiff competition. These rankings correlate quite strongly with per capita income. . . .

Economic Freedom Promotes Unity

Economic freedom breeds not just prosperity; it breeds also a sense of belonging to a global community surrounded by trading partners, as opposed to an insular community surrounded by enemies. Singapore, for example, is politically repressed but economically free, and it is a good and prosperous citizen of the world.

Last week [in October 2001], I gave a public lecture where a member of the audience (whom I wish I could credit by name) summed it all up in a sentence: We need to think less about nation-building and more about economy-building. Or even more succinctly: It's the economy, stupid. If Afghanistan is ever to recover, it will be not through legislatures and political parties, but through free markets, enforceable property rights, and international trade.

Right now, the freest countries in the Middle East are Jordan and Egypt, both of which rank ahead of Israel on the Fraser Institute's economic freedom scale. They're now tied for 52nd place (out of 116), after having ranked 67th and 88th just 10 years ago. Egypt's spectacular improvement is due to lower government spending, the repeal of price controls, lower marginal tax rates, a more stable monetary policy, improvements in the legal system designed to protect property rights, lower tariffs, and new freedoms to transact with foreigners and hold foreign currency. We should be thinking about ways to encourage and replicate these tentative moves toward free market economies, not only in Afghanistan but in economically repressive countries like Saudi Arabia, which are proving to be breeding grounds for terrorism.

"If you want to lift people out of starvation, political freedom is a luxury. Economic freedom is a necessity."

So how do we encourage economic freedom? Well, how do you encourage *anything?* The first thing that comes to mind is bribery—economic assistance that's contingent on the maintenance of free institutions. What I'm proposing is that when we're setting our conditions, we should focus more on economic institutions than on political ones.

We can also reward foreign economic development by opening our own borders to trade. This is an experiment we've never really tried in America, where the book-length NAFTA [North American Free Trade Agreement] treaty passes for a "free trade" agreement. A *true* free trade policy would fit on the back of an envelope, and it would say that the United States will levy no tariffs, impose no import quotas, and take no action (except as justified by national security) to interfere with the free flow of goods across our borders. Though it would be a tough sell politically, we know from economic theory that such a policy would enrich both Americans and non-Americans. Even more important, it would give every citizen of the Third World a stake in America's survival and America's prosperity. And of course it would make the world a freer place, which is exactly what this fight is all about.

Authoritarianism Is the Best System for Afghanistan

by Robert J. Barro

About the author: *Robert J. Barro is a senior fellow at the Hoover Institution and the Robert C. Waggoner Professor of Economics at Harvard University. His published works include* Getting It Right: Market Choices in a Free Society *and* Nothing Is Sacred: Economic Ideas for the New Millennium.

The military successes in Afghanistan have demonstrated the awesome technological prowess of U.S. air power. However, as the campaign evolves into a nation-building operation, we shall find that our skills in the social and political arena do not match our military talents. The U.S. vision for a postwar Afghanistan relies on the familiar recipes of democracy and massive foreign aid. Unfortunately, neither is likely to work effectively.

Education Levels Are Too Low

The Western ideal for representative democracy involves free, multiparty elections and maintenance of civil liberties. As Aristotle realized, and as the evidence from a large number of countries demonstrates, democracy is almost never sustained in a country that has income and education levels as low as those in Afghanistan. Nevertheless, Washington always recommends democracy, even to the poorest nations, and the results have included such failures as the new Congo and Haiti.

[The human rights agency] Freedom House's latest ratings place Afghanistan in the lowest categories for electoral rights and civil liberties. This lack of democracy corresponds to the predictions that I would make from the country's economic and social conditions. Given where Afghanistan is today, my statistical analysis implies that the chance a midrange democracy—characteristic at present of countries such as Turkey and Indonesia—will exist five years from now is less than 1 percent.

A major factor undermining the building of democracy in Afghanistan is low primary school attainment. In 1995, adults had an average of 0.8 years of formal schooling. Only Mali and Niger were lower among the 113 countries for which I have data. Even worse from the standpoint of democracy is the unequal treatment of males and females. In Afghanistan, adult males averaged 1.3 years of primary schooling, whereas females had only 0.3. The male-female ratio of 4.3 is the highest for the 104 countries for which I have these data. The next highest is for Pakistan, which had 1.8 years for males and 0.6 for females. However, poor treatment of women does not apply only to Islamic countries. For example, many non-Muslim countries in Africa also have very high ratios of male-to-female schooling. . . .

> *"The U.S. vision for a postwar Afghanistan relies on the familiar recipes of democracy and massive foreign aid. . . . Neither is likely to work effectively."*

Authoritarianism Is the Better Option

The lesson for the Bush administration is that the United States ought not to plan for a postwar Afghanistan that has functioning democratic institutions. A more realistic plan would focus on finding, or at least accepting, an efficient authoritarian regime that would provide political stability and improve economic conditions. Power sharing among local factions may conceivably be part of the picture, but the stability of this arrangement is doubtful for a country with Afghanistan's large number of fragmented ethnic groups.

Ethnic heterogeneity is a source of political instability in Afghanistan. A possible solution, probably too radical for Washington to contemplate, is to partition Afghanistan into several independent countries as a way to achieve greater homogeneity within each political jurisdiction. However, the transition to multiple states can itself promote violence, as is clear from the former Yugoslavia.

The Pitfalls of Foreign Aid

Foreign aid is a critical issue as well. Given the dire economic conditions in Afghanistan, a large amount of short-term assistance makes sense. The problem is that short-term help tends to evolve into long-term aid, which historically has *not* contributed to economic development. Instead of alleviating poverty or promoting economic growth, foreign aid has tended to sustain large, corrupt governments.

[U.S. political scientist] William Easterly argues in his recent book, *The Elusive Quest for Growth*, that the problem is not foreign aid per se but rather the way in which aid programs relate to past performance. Basically, to qualify for American aid, a country has to mess things up. The reward for success is that a country "graduates" and becomes ineligible for future aid. The currently fashionable debt-relief programs work essentially in the same way. Easterly argues that the policy formula should be reversed: "As countries' incomes rise because of their favorable policies for economic growth, aid should increase in matching fashion." Unfortunately, aid givers are unlikely to adopt this hardheaded approach. In fact, Easterly's own reward for publicizing this and other radical reform proposals was to be encouraged to leave his research position at the World Bank.

The likelihood is that entrenched foreign aid will become part of Afghanistan's problems, rather than a piece of the solution. We can already see how warlords are stealing much of the grain being sent, bolstering their positions in the country. This will only get worse over time.

Someday, perhaps, we will become as hardheaded about the war on world poverty as we have become about the war on international terrorism. But for now, we seem to be relying on the soft weapons of democracy and foreign aid, policies that have failed time and again.

An Islamic State Is Best for Afghanistan

by Yusuf Patel

About the author: *Yusuf Patel, a respected Islamic scholar born in India, lives in Toronto, Canada, where he is a religious leader of the Muslim community.*

Since [the terrorist attack on America on] September 11 [2001], two forms of attack were accelerated against the Islamic Umah [brotherhood] and the Islamic Ruling System (The Khilafah[1]):

1. *Physical Attack:* Which took the form of military attack both launched straight away such as against Afghanistan and the intention to attack others was declared, such as the recent calls to attack Iraq.[2]

2. *Intellectual Attack:* This is always the less open attack, and therefore the most dangerous. This is the attack that I will Insha Allah [God willing] focus upon. A number of attacks have been levelled against the Muslims since September 11.

A large number of which focused upon the ability of Islam to solve contemporary problems built around the false premise that the application of Islam upon a society leads to inevitable conflicts [and] oppression of Women. . . .

James Rubin, the former assistant secretary of state under [President Bill] Clinton wrote in an article in the *Independent* [on October 14, 2001]:

> We must send a clear and simple message to the Muslim world. If Osama bin Laden's vision were achieved, all of the Islamic world would look like Afghanistan under the Taliban. Do you really want to live in Bin Laden Land, a Stone Age Islamic caliphate with no rights, no economy and no future?

When applied upon a people, Islam would lead society to economic, political stagnation, the state would have to be ruled by the iron fist to stop the people

---

1. The Khilafah is the 'Islamic State' according to the Koran, the Muslim holy book. It refers to the global leadership of all Muslims in the world.   2. The United States invaded Iraq in 2003 and deposed dictator Saddam Hussein.

from rebelling, in the picture painted so vividly by James Rubin.

Also, Tariq Ali, born a Muslim but adopted Trotskyism (Communism according to the sacred tenets of Leon Trotsky) whilst studying at Oxford [University in Oxford, United Kingdom] described Islam 'as a stagnant, backward-looking and disastrously factionalized culture badly in need of its own Reformation'.

The self-proclaimed Trotskyist argues that the Muslims need to seriously look to reforming Islam, updating it to fit the modern realities of the twenty-first Century.

Just as Microsoft updates its operating system in order to fit with the needs of its consumers, easily shifting from Windows 3.1 to Windows 95, 98, 2000 to Windows XP, Islam needs to follow the same course in reality to become palatable to the taste of the West.

The Italian PM [prime minister] Berlusconi said, "We must be aware of the superiority of our civilisation, a system that has guaranteed—in contrast with Islamic countries—respect for religious and political rights".

Mr Berlusconi well known for his financial probity and business ethics, in a statement reminiscent of [Francis] Fukuyama [a political economist at Johns Hopkins University] trumpets the superiority of Western Civilisation, which stands at odds with the 'Islamic Countries' which he erroneously describes as the carriers and guardians of Islam.

It is very easy in this post 9-11 world for the West to celebrate the end of History with the claim that the Capitalist System represents the pinnacle of human history.

Surely bringing back the Khilafah (Caliphate) is an endeavour doomed to failure, hasn't the 'Islamic experiment' failed in Sudan, Iran, Saudi Arabia and Afghanistan?

All of these countries to one degree or another sought rapprochement with the West which ultimately led them to be dependent upon the West to varying degrees.

A number of these acts of intellectual slander have been levied upon the Islamic Ruling System (the Khilafah) by the Western nations which hope by portraying Islam as a backward culture, it would deter the Muslims from working towards its re-establishment.

It is important in this context to peel away the layers of such lies as well as to show the uniqueness and superiority of the Islamic Ruling System, whilst refraining from taking such a defensive stance with regards

> *"A large number of [attacks that] focused . . . on the ability of Islam to solve contemporary problems [were] built around the false premise that . . . Islam . . . leads to inevitable conflicts."*

to Islam, so as to change its intrinsic nature as laid down by Allah (Subhanahu Wa Ta'aala) [God] through his beloved Rasool (Sallallahu Alaihi Wasallam) [the Prophet Muhammad].

It is also important to take the intellectual attacks back to the West.

Why should we be on the defensive concerning Islam, when we can all witness the rotten fruits of Western Civilisation on a daily basis.

Attacks on Islam

[Some] specific attacks include the following:
1. The Islamic Ruling System is a dictatorship.
2. Islam subjugates Women. . . .

It is essential for the Islamic Ummah to realise the danger in trying to distort Islam or to dilute its true essence. Islam is a trust upon the shoulders of its guardians whose responsibility once evaluated will lead either to happiness or profound regret depending upon how this responsibility was discharged, this will be felt on the Day of Hashr (accountability).

The Islamic Ruling System Is a Dictatorship

The future of Islam lies with democracy and freedom. [Iran] where a real democracy is taking shape with [President] Ayatollah Mohamad Khatami could set a model for an Islamic state. . . . One has to free Islam from decadence, from the Taliban, from damaging beliefs inherited from our ancestors, from those who, for example, say that Islam is against democracy, against the freedom of women, against arts, against free elections, against dialogue between civilisations . . . against those who pretend that because we are Muslims, we must invade others and impose our faith upon the whole world. Rashed Ghannoushi, (exiled leader of the Tunisian outlawed "Al-Da'wa" Party) in an interview titled 'Freeing Islam from the Taliban', *Al-Ahram Weekly*, 1–7 October 1998.

The mistaken logical assumptions of those who claim Islam to be in harmony with Democracy fall into two distinct traps.

A Misapplication of the rule of opposites linked to a profound failure to comprehend the reality of Democracy. If the Islamic State is not democratic it must be a tyrannical dictatorship. It certainly does not fit comfortably with the framework of dictatorial rule therefore it must be democratic, right? Wrong.

Such logical deductions fail to comprehend the fact that it can be—and is in actuality—at odds with the essence of Democratic rule. The Democratic system is built around the premise that the people are the Source of all laws, they must decide how their lives are governed, this places man in the drivers seat in deciding how life should be organised in terms or rules and laws. From the point of view of Islam, Allah (Subhanhu Wa Ta'aala) is the creator and legislator, he defines how we must live our lives and not man. This does not mean the Islamic system is a dictatorship.

Elections Serve a Different Purpose in Islam and Democracy

Elections are style permitted by the Shar'iah [Islamic law] in principle. Within the Khilafah state it is a permitted means by which to elect a Khaleefah [Head] for the Muslims, and to elect representatives to the Majlis Al-Ummah (The

People's Assembly) which will decide matters related to the implementation of some practical issues related to domestic matters in ruling, education, health, trading, industry, farming and the like, it has full powers to account [to] the rulers within the Khilafah, and it has the right to voice discontent of Waalis (Governors) which the Khaleefah is bound by, and has to remove them if demanded by the Majlis.

Democracy utilises the style of elections in order to choose representatives who in turn legislate rules and laws for the people. The fact that the Islamic Ruling System and Democracy utilise the style of elections should not be a means by which to infer a similarity, the objective behind the utilisation of such a style is completely different.

> "It is important . . . to show the uniqueness and superiority of the Islamic Ruling System."

The Khaleefah must be selected by consent and not by force. If a Khaleefah takes power without consent he would be classed as a Mutasallit (Usurper) and his immediate removal is obliged upon the Ummah as it is classed as a Munkar (evil).

[The Islamic theologian] Al-Bukhari reported on the authority of Ibn Abbas [cousin of Muhammad, the Prophet of Islam] who said:

> . . . Abdur-Rahman [one of the first converts in Islam in the seventh century] came to me and said, "Would that you had seen the man who came today to the Chief of the Believers ('Umar), saying, 'O Chief of the Believers! What do you think about so-and-so who says, 'If 'Umar [seventh-century Khaleefah] should die, I will give the pledge of allegiance to such-and-such person . . .'

> 'Umar became angry and then said, 'Allah willing, I will stand before the people tonight and warn them against those people who want to deprive the others of their rights (the question of rulership).'

This happened during the Haj [pilgrimage to Mecca] season. Abdur-Rahman convinced him that he should delay his speech until he arrives to Medina [where prophet Muhammad was born]. Umar having arrived in Medina addressed the people with the following words:

> (O people!) I have been informed that a speaker amongst you says, 'By Allah, if 'Umar should die, I will give the pledge of allegiance to such-and-such person.' . . . Remember that whoever gives the pledge of allegiance to anybody among you without consulting the other Muslims, neither that person, nor the person to whom the pledge of allegiance was given, are to be supported, lest they both should be killed.

Umar made clear to the people that the leader cannot be imposed by force, and if he is he ought to be killed, as it is the taking of a right away from the people acknowledged by the Ahkam Shar'iah [Islamic laws] as such.

Due to the public nature of the address, and the speaking out against this practice, this counts as evidence as the Sahabah [the companion of Muhammad the prophet] remained silent to it which is indicative of approval, therefore this counts as Ijma As-Sahabah (consensus of the companions).

Therefore the Bai'ah [a symbolic contract between the leader and the people of an Islamic state] needs to be enacted by the majority and without coercion.

Poor US Record with Democracy

The Western Nations claim to adopt democracy, upholding it throughout the globe, and singing its praises at every given opportunity. Doesn't the World's leading nation claim to be the land of 'Freedom and Democracy' (. . . And Milk and Honey?). Let us look to their recent record.

[During the 2000 presidential election] in Florida, the home of the 'pregnant chads' (controversial voting papers not rate of illegitimate births), the Republican Party Machine disenfranchised 57,000 voters for the simple reason that they were proven Democratic Party voters, and coincidentally African-American. They were left off the voter lists purposefully under the pretext of criminal records which is a bar to voting in Florida. The simple fact is that none of the 57,000 African Americans had criminal records just voting records which the Republican Party saw as a hindrance to 'stealing the presidency'. Indeed the Secretary of State for Florida, Katherine Harris, who was the arbiter for the election and over-saw the election process, was the Campaign chairwoman for [George W.] Bush's Presidential election campaign, no conflict of interest there [Bush won]!

This is unsurprising as America claims Democracy to be sacrosanct, but is more than willing to sacrifice it on the altar of interest. In April of this year [2002], Hugo Chavez the 'democratically elected' leader of Venezuela was unseated by a Coup D'etat supported by the Bush Administration. It was the US State department which falsely claimed that Chavez had resigned, this was disseminated by all major US television Networks and Newspapers. The *New York Times* in an editorial openly supported the Coup plotters. The Paragon of US factual programming trusted as an unquestionable source of integrity by the US public justified the Coup on the basis that Chavez was a 'nut' and a 'communist' to boot, who was unpopular and a dictator.

> *"[The Islamic State] does not fit comfortably with the framework of dictatorial rule therefore it must be democratic, right? Wrong."*

The *New York Times* wrote, "Venezuelan democracy is no longer threatened by a would-be dictator . . . [because] the military intervened and handed power to a respected business leader."

[According to] Philip T. Reeker, Deputy Spokesman for the State Department stated on April 12, 2002: "essential elements of democracy . . . have been weakened in recent months."

Since Chavez was returned to power after two days, the evidence of planning by Washington traces complicity back several months before the coup took place.

The US supported the overthrow of 'democratically elected' governments throughout its post–Second World War history. Although the corruption on the government of [Pakistan's former president] Nawaz Sharif was well known, the US supported the ousting of its 'elected' government by General Pervez Musharraf whose rigged Referendum campaign was welcomed by the same President [George W. Bush] who entered office through dubious means. The US supports a string of dictators and unelected thugs throughout the Islamic World, illustrating the subservience of sacred principles where US national interest collides. The Same applies to all Capitalist Nations to one degree or another, although the status of the US as principal hegemon makes her transgressions more pronounced. . . .

Islam Subjugates Women

Western academics, politicians, journalists and Feminists as well as their counterparts in the Muslim Countries seek to label Islam with labels such as Misogynist, oppressive and cruel as a slur on Islam's treatment of Women. An often repeated stance of the Muslims is to take a defensive stand which is often tantamount to conceding the superiority of Capitalism in the treatment of women. Islam emanates from the creator who is in the best position to define the roles of both Men and Women. The present Capitalist system in the West has failed to truly define the role of either gender and has in the process popularised 'the war of the sexes', to the extent that Women are led to believe success translates into career, to the level that motherhood is almost frowned upon. A Woman has not achieved 'life's goals' unless she has had a career. Governments often send cross signals by offering incentives to have children and then childcare policies which encourage the parents to leave the child with a stranger whilst the parents are at work, thereby consigning the formative years of a child to a paid employee.

Any system primarily educates via its popular mediums, the popular mediums in the west are the Television and magazines/Newspapers. They disseminate the ideas which mould general behaviour. The disproportionate depiction of Women as objects of Sexual desire elevate the base desires. Women have to therefore conform to the image pre-determined for them on the whole by Men. The impact of these ideas so closely associated with the general acceptance of Freedom cause severe problems to the social fabric of society. A recent report commissioned by the Home Office in Britain determined that one in 20 Women have been victims of rape, and the majority of these rapes are inflicted by men who the victims knows, only 8% are raped by a stranger. In the Islamic Khilafah, the principal duties and rights are determined by the Legislator, Allah (Subhanahu Wa

> *"America claims Democracy to be sacrosanct, but is more than willing to sacrifice it on the altar of interest."*

Ta'aala), and not by man. The Principal role of the woman is as a mother and a wife, although there is no bar to involvement in public life whether that be economic or political. She can work, but this cannot be at the expense of her duties to her husband and children. She can be a member of the Majlis Al-Ummah (The People's Assembly), a judge or a Civil Servant.

Islam Respects Women

Firstly, Allah (Subhanahu Wa Ta'aala) addressed Insan (Humankind) with obligations which will be subject to accountability on Yawm Al-Hashr (Day of Accountability). Both Man and Woman are equal in the sight of Allah (Subhanahu Wa Ta'aala) inasmuch that they both possess the propensity to think and both are vital to achieve the continuation of the Human race.

Islam forbade the free-mixing between the sexes and prohibits Khulwa (Seclusion) which enables the crime of rape which pervades Western society to be conducted so easily. It also puts a halt to the dissemination of ideas of sexual freedom and imagery, it also honours the status of Women by not treating her as a commodity or a sexual instrument. Indeed the Khilafah system will seek to change the ideas which shape the relations between Men and Women, so that Marriage be the institution which binds them both together and not promiscuous sexual encounters which lead to the cheapening of human interaction.

The crime statistics related to Women are an indictment upon the 'guardians of freedom and democracy'.

- In the USA 1.3 women are raped every minute, this translates into 78 rapes each hour, 1872 rapes each day, 56160 rapes each month and 683,280 rapes per year (Statistics from the National Victim Centre, NVC)
- 1 out of every 3 American woman will be sexually assaulted in her lifetime (NVC)
- 1 in 4 college women have either been raped or suffered attempted rape (NVC)
- In 1998 there were 3,170,520 arrests of women, of which 272,073 were drug related (US State Department, 1999)
- A woman is beaten every 15 seconds by her partner, it happens at some time in 25%–35% of American homes (FBI)
- 77 women die from abusive partners every week, which is 4000 a year (FBI).
- The BBC reported that nearly 25% of women in the UK face domestic violence at some stage in their life. Police are called to an incident of domestic violence every 60 seconds and receive 1,300 calls each day related to this. Domestic violence kills two women each week in the UK.

If we study the ultimate form of dishonour that a woman can experience, that of rape, we find shocking statistics illustrating the reality. In the US, a rape occurs every minute, and in the UK, one-third of women have been sexually abused by the age of 18. Also, there was a 500% increase in the reporting of rape between 1996 and 1997. In addition, the sentence for rape can be as low as 180 hours community service.

Afghanistan Should Be Reconstructed as an Islamic Democracy

by Luke Thomas

About the author: *Luke Thomas is a writer and fellow at the Digital Freedom Network, a U.S. nonprofit agency that seeks to promote human rights, limited government, the rule of law, and individual freedom.*

The *New York Times* reports that on January 4 [2004], "Delegates at a national meeting approved a new Constitution for Afghanistan on Sunday, concluding three weeks of often tense debate. Their decision heralded a new era of democracy after a quarter-century of war."

According to reports, Afghanistan will be renamed the Islamic Republic of Afghanistan in its effort to "combine democracy and religion." Elections will be held in six months within the newly-created democratic presidential system, including directly elected president and a two-chamber national assembly (one chamber will be the Wolsei Jirga or "house of people" and the other chamber will be Meshrano Jirga or "house of elders"). An independent judiciary has also been created.

Civil rights of religious minorities are afforded legal protection and women are given special consideration: women are recognized as equal citizens before the law and 25 percent of the seats in the national legislature are allocated for them.

Interestingly, the document is thoroughly Islamic: Islam has been declared the state's official and "sacred religion", no law can be contrary to the beliefs and practices of Islam, and in addition to the notable name change to the "Islamic Republic of Afghanistan", the new flag contains a prayer niche and pulpit with two inscribed Islamic core ideological tenets, "There is no God but Allah and Muhammed is his Prophet" and "Allah Akbar" ("God is Great").

Thus, the conflation of robust Islam with democracy seems to have created an

"Islamic democracy." But is such a moniker a contradiction within its own definitional parameters? Traditional arguments have viewed Islam as diametrically opposed to democracy (arguments have even been extended to suggest that Islam and oppressive systems of government have a wide swathe of overlapping characteristics. To be certain, there are elements of both entities that resemble each other, i.e. are both "oppressive" in some form. However, a major Abrahamic religion and various theoretical systems of governments are so radically incomparable that any resemblance must be inept, largely contrived, coincidental if at all true, and likely of no substantive value). The *Christian Science Monitor* summarizes the argument against combining Islam and democracy:

> *"There are significant elements in Islam that facilitate its inclusion into and compatibility with life in a democracy."*

> Islam, the argument goes, breeds a submissive attitude—not only to Allah but also to political and religious leaders as well—that makes Muslims inherently incapable of participating in the rough-and-tumble world of electoral politics and of respecting the rights of minorities who follow a different religious or cultural path.

The dilemma is that if such assessments accurately capture "authentic" Islam, then democracy can never take root in such societies. If true, the US has embarked on monumental wastes of time. Even without in-depth analysis, in at least the 20th century Islamic societies have neither adopted effective capitalist policies nor have they been remotely respective of human rights. Presently, there is widespread abuse in the name of Islam towards women, religious and ethnic minorities and foreign territories and governments. Abhorrence and violence by Muslims "for Islam" is a fact. Although enormously regrettable, it is nevertheless a reality that cannot be ignored.

Islam Is Compatible with Democracy

However, such inapplicable and clumsy generalizations that Muslims are wide-eyed fatalistically driven creatures who are beyond reason and beneficial mutations are fortunately incorrect. The U.S. is acting very appropriately in fostering democracy throughout the Middle East.

There exists the tendency to extrapolate out of Islam's history inherent deficiencies, penchants for violence, bigotry and unmitigated loathing by Muslims for all things "not Muslim". These abstractions are entirely unjustified as they do not take into account differing histories, governmental policies, literature, trends, common beliefs, philosophical disputes, locations of acceptance and alternative cultural instantiations that are all required to gain an adequate perspective of "Islam." How is one to make sense of a survey of Egyptians, Iranians, Moroccans, Bosnians and Indonesians? In such a sample, the coherence of the group falls apart on fundamental levels, most notably on cultural grounds. One cannot reduce Muslims to nothing more than their religion since myriad other factors also shape their views and lives.

It is also unclear that the aforementioned problems Islam faces are somehow unique to Islam and not issues all religions must or have resolved. Therefore, to define "Islam" as merely "Islam" without incorporating substantial discontinuities and important nuances that are historical, philosophical, and cultural in nature, one cannot possibly expect to garner an accurate portrayal of what Islam truly is: an unbelievably intricate, widespread and powerful religion affecting billions of followers in incalculably different ways (there are important core ideological and historical similarities, some more important than others, such as Muhammed as the prophet of God, but the point is that an entity as daedal as "Islam" is fantastically involved and requires erudition to accurately grasp).

The acknowledgement of these discontinuities is imperative. The gaps in knowledge about Islam are misunderstandings concerning genuine beliefs. Islam, contrary to what is often presented, has significant values and teachings that are absolutely crucial to and necessary for democracy.

Professor Noah Feldman of New York University contends that Islam is a fluid and mobile idea that carries different meanings in different cultures and universal truths alike. But he firmly holds that in Islam, all humans are equal before God and the law and that each person has responsibilities to society. Feldman argues Islam makes paramount the notion that human beings should be treated with respect and that they must treat others likewise. World-renowned Middle East scholar Bernard Lewis echoes this sentiment:

> But beyond these there are older traditions, well represented in both the political literature and political experience of the Islamic Middle East: traditions of government under the law, by consent, even by contract . . . the rejection by the traditional jurists of despotic and arbitrary rule in favor of contract in the formation and consensus in the conduct of government; and their insistence that the mightiest of rulers, no less than the humblest of his servants, is bound by the law.

Lewis adds that a further complementary element of Islam is the requirement of tolerance by quoting the Koranic verse "there is no compulsion in religion" and "diversity in my community is God's mercy." Also, there is the Sufi ideal of dialogue among the faiths in an attempt to fulfill their mutual aspirations.

"Whatever forms these Middle Eastern democracies take, they must evolve slowly and create a future of their own accord."

What Lewis and Feldman are suggesting is not that Islam is faultless and without significant problems; both unequivocally agree it has disconcerting issues. Both are seeking to demonstrate there are significant elements in Islam that facilitate its inclusion into and compatibility with life in a democracy.

Challenges to Democracy

Given that these notions of compatibility are true, how does an Islamic democracy work?

Feldman argues the process is not easy. He first underscores that Middle Eastern Muslims have a natural fear of secular governments since they have historically been the most repressive regimes in the Middle East. Concurrently, devout "Islamists", or politically minded hard-line Muslims, are untainted by scandal and are "steadfast in challenging autocracy." Thus, "[the Islamists] speak the language of the people."

For any democracy to function, a civil society must be both in place

> *"The path to democracy through Islam is new, uncharted and full of uncertainties."*

and active. In any contemporary Islamic democracy, Islamists will primarily fill that role. Secular governments have never made Islam illegal, but traditional political parties have been outlawed. The mosque will likely be the focal point for "organization, recruitment and advertising." Islamists will dominate the short and medium run of Islamic democracies.

This near monopolization of politics and political office by those whose interests are anathema to democratic ideals (or at least Western conceptions of them) is possible. After achieving their goals by attaining real power, these Islamists could then decide to abolish elections and impose their vision of theocracy. Feldman and Lewis believe this is unquestionably a valid concern.

Democracy could also collapse if the U.S. too closely attempts to transplant its secularized democracy. Feldman observes that, "nothing could delegitimize a constitution more quickly than America setting down secularist red lines in a well-meaning show of neo-imperialism." Both Lewis and Feldman agree that whatever forms these Middle Eastern democracies take, they must evolve slowly and create a future of their own accord.

Few Alternatives to Democracy

Even if one is skeptical about the likelihood of success, what is the alternative? President [George W.] Bush keenly noted that America has for too long allowed grievous regimes in the Middle East to exist out of concerns for stability. Permitting authoritarian regimes to abrogate their citizens' rights has not worked in our (and clearly not in their, meaning the people of those regimes) favor. Moreover, denying democracy to the Middle East will play right into the hands of the Islamic radicals who will desperately attempt to show their religion and freedom cannot feasibly unite. The solution, therefore, is to "persuade a majority of the world's 1.2 billion Muslims that Islam and democracy are perfectly compatible," says Feldman. That task is not as difficult as it may seem. Experts across the region universally acknowledge that there has been importuning from numerous Middle Eastern residents for some level of democratization.

The U.S. must also foster economic prosperity and social stability to these new governments. While on the one hand the U.S. must release its grip on Afghanistan and Iraq, on the other it must take responsibility for helping to raise living standards and eliminating overbearing security threats from terrorists or warlords. There will be absolute futility in these democratization efforts if the U.S. commands these fledgling governments to sink or swim without having taught them to operate in these new and precarious environments.

Lewis captures all of these preceding ideas and arguments succinctly:

> The study of Islamic history and of the vast and rich Islamic political literature encourages the belief that it may well be possible to develop democratic institutions—not necessarily in our Western definition of that much misused term, but in one deriving from their own history and culture, and ensuring, in their way, limited government under law, consultation and openness, in a civilized and humane society. There is enough in the traditional culture of Islam on the one hand and the modern experience of the Muslim peoples on the other to provide the basis for an advance towards freedom in the true sense of that word.

The path to democracy through Islam is new, uncharted and full of uncertainties. In truth, no one (including this writer) is certain whether or not they will succeed and achieve the desired democratic ends. Yet, the overarching point is that there is justified and ample reason to believe they can. With serious, disciplined and concerted efforts, worshippers of Islam will finally be able to share the experience of freedom as maintained by themselves, for their nations and through their faith.

Implementing Democracy Too Soon in Afghanistan Is Dangerous

by Michael Massing

About the author: *Former executive editor of* Columbia Journalism, *Michael Massing writes for the* New York Times *and is author of* The Fix, *a study of U.S. drug policy since the 1960s.*

From Washington to London to Bonn, it's now an article of faith that building a nation means creating a Western-style democracy. That is certainly the case with Afghanistan. The industrialized nations that recently promised $4.5 billion to help rebuild the country all assume that it will adopt Western political institutions. And the Afghans themselves have agreed on a political blueprint that calls for a transitional government ending in "free and fair elections" within 30 months.

But a growing group of experts caution against introducing too much democracy too fast in failed states. "There is a democratic template that, once put in place, requires you to focus resources on things that aren't essential," said Thomas Carothers, the vice president for studies at the Carnegie Endowment for International Peace. Elections, for instance, "require a huge amount of work," he said. "You have to concentrate very early on the development of political parties. That takes a lot of time and training. Then you have to educate people. And you have to arrange for media messages, via radio. And you have to train 10,000 to 15,000 election observers." This, Mr. Carothers said, diverts attention from providing more immediate basic services essential to making people's day-to-day lives more livable.

Aside from being a distraction, elections can also encourage conflict, especially in countries where arms remain rampant. "There's a large literature showing that with democratization, you're more likely to have violence," said Susan Woodward, a professor of political science at the City University of New York

Graduate Center. Early elections, she said, strengthen people who are armed, like warlords, for they can use their weapons to confront opponents and intimidate voters.

In Cambodia, national elections were held two years after the signing of the United Nations supervised cease-fire in 1991. But the forces under the control of the strongman Hun Sen remained armed, and, despite losing the election, he got himself installed as a shadow prime minister. In 1997, he seized full power in a coup. Earlier this year [2002], as Cambodia was preparing to hold its first local elections in decades, 20 opposition candidates and activists were killed, and Hun Sen's party, benefiting from the intimidation, won control of all but 20 of 1,621 communal councils.

In the new Russian federation, the government devoted much energy to holding elections, setting up political parties and establishing a parliament in December 1991, after the Soviet Union collapsed. But it neglected the urgent task of strengthening the state institutions that had withered under communism, said Stephen Kotkin, a professor at Princeton and the author of "Armageddon Averted: The Soviet Collapse, 1970–2000." "On Jan. 1, 1992, Russia had its own flag, a multiparty system, competitive elections and many civic associations," Mr. Kotkin said. "But it was the semblance, rather than the reality, of democracy. The country had 6,000 judges and 250,000 K.G.B. agents." What Russia really needed, he added, was not elections and parties but an improved judiciary, a stronger bureaucracy and enhanced regulatory agencies—"all the things that were out of favor in the 1990's."

A Poor Record of Democratization

This stress on democratization began in the 1980's. The Reagan administration, seeking to combat communism, promoted Western-style institutions in countries under authoritarian rule. Specialists in the American way of governance fanned out to places like El Salvador, Haiti, Poland and Czechoslovakia, helping to establish opposition parties, finance independent newspapers and monitor elections.

With the dissolution of the Soviet Union, many nations that had been propped up by Washington or Moscow were suddenly abandoned, and some collapsed. As Gerald Helman, a retired Foreign Service officer, and Steven R. Ratner, a fellow at the Council on Foreign Relations, wrote in the journal *Foreign Policy* in 1992, "From Haiti in the Western Hemisphere to the remnants of Yugoslavia in Europe, from Somalia, Sudan and Liberia in Africa to Cambodia in Southeast Asia, a disturbing new phenomenon is emerging: the failed nation-state, utterly incapable of sustaining itself as a member of the international community."

> *"A growing group of experts caution against introducing too much democracy too fast in failed states."*

Traditional responses like more bilateral aid, they argued, were inadequate. In nations that retained a minimal government structure, it was fine to promote democracy, but in those that had fully collapsed, "a more intrusive form" of intervention was warranted, with the United Nations taking over many government functions.

In the 1990's, as crises broke out in places like Somalia, Haiti and Bosnia, the Clinton administration kept the emphasis on democratization. Thus, in Bosnia, a country torn apart by bitter ethnic rivalries, the 1995 Dayton accord [that ended the Bosnian war] called for elections in 10 months.

But existing political groups proved adept at exploiting them, and according to Morton Abramowitz, a former United States ambassador and a board member of the International Crisis Group, which has been monitoring the implementation of Dayton, the elections served mainly to "solidify the power of the most nationalistic elements."

One country that has had a more positive experience is Mozambique. There, as elsewhere, elections were scheduled soon after the end of a civil war. But in the two years before they were held, steps were taken to convert Renamo, the rebel army, into a political force. Terrence Lyons, a professor at the Institute for Conflict Analysis and Resolution at George Mason University, said that "the international community, led by the Italians, determined that if Renamo was to play a political role, it had to have the resources to do it. So it was provided offices, volunteers, telephones and faxes. Renamo was given training in how to hold rallies and put out newsletters."

> *"The Reagan administration, seeking to combat communism, promoted Western-style institutions in countries under authoritarian rule."*

At the same time, the presence of 7,500 peacekeepers in the country made it hard for Renamo to continue pursuing power through the barrel of a gun. Today, Mozambique's democracy remains incomplete, and the state weak, but the country is at peace. "After many years in which people were afraid to visit their grandparents 10 miles away because of bandits on the road, now they can," Mr. Lyons said. "That there's not a collapsed state or anarchy is a significant achievement."

Afghanistan faces a similar challenge in dealing with its armed factions. At a recent debate on Afghan reconstruction at the Carnegie Endowment in Washington, Marina Ottaway, a senior associate at the Endowment, argued that the rush to embrace a "democratic reconstruction model" for Afghanistan is "dangerous," creating unrealistically high expectations.

The plan to hold early elections, while "well-intentioned," she said, ignores the strength of the warlords. Afghanistan's "highly decentralized, quasi-medieval system," Ms. Ottaway went on, required a more "pragmatic" approach in which the international community works with the warlords to distribute aid in regions where the central government is weak.

That is the wrong approach, insisted Paula Newberg, a special adviser to the United Nations Foundation who has traveled frequently to Afghanistan in recent years. The warlords have "abysmally low support," she maintained, adding that Afghanistan "deserves the efforts of the international community to build it as close to the standard of a contemporary state as it can."

> *"To some degree, the debate over . . . how much emphasis to place on democracy is really about timing."*

That outside world, she added, "cannot tolerate corruption, concessions to warlords, or the sacrifice of any Afghan aspirations to democracy."

The Debate Is over Timing

To some degree, the debate over how to handle the warlords, and how much emphasis to place on democracy, is really about timing. Both pessimists like Ms. Ottaway and optimists like Ms. Newberg agree that if any type of stability is to be achieved in war-shattered countries like Afghanistan, a climate of security must first be achieved. "Law and order must be the first priority," said Morton Halperin, who directed the policy planning staff in the State Department under President Bill Clinton and who now directs the Open Society Institute's office in Washington. "The main thing is developing a capacity to help a country through a transitional period in a way that allows a democratic process to take hold."

Unfortunately, Mr. Halperin said, this does not seem to be happening in Afghanistan. In contrast to Bosnia, where 60,000 peacekeepers were initially stationed, only 3,500 have been sent to Afghanistan, a country 12 times as large. Just this week [February 2002], the Central Intelligence Agency itself warned in a classified report that Afghanistan could again plunge into chaos if steps were not taken to restrain and disarm rival warlords.

In all the talk about nation-building, peacekeeping is often seen as an afterthought. But it may turn out to be a precondition, making everything else—including democracy—possible.

Organizations to Contact

The editor has compiled the following list of organizations concerned with the issues debated in this book. The descriptions are derived from materials provided by the organizations. All have publications or information available for interested readers. The list was compiled on the date of publication of the present volume; names, addresses, and phone numbers may change. Be aware that many organizations take several weeks or longer to respond to inquiries, so allow as much time as possible.

Afghanistan Foundation
209 Pennsylvania Ave. SE, Suite 700, Washington, DC 20003
(202) 543-1177
e-mail: info@afghanistanfoundation.org • Web site: www.afghanistanfoundation.org

The Afghanistan Foundation was set up in 1996 as a partnership between Americans and Afghans designed to bring peace, stability, and prosperity to Afghanistan, and to reduce confrontation in central and south Asia. To further these objectives, the foundation has a number of projects including the Afghanistan Charter Project, which brings together Afghan scholars and leaders from around the world to discuss how to establish a democratic government in Afghanistan. In another major project, a senior task force, which includes U.S. senators and Afghan government officials, was set up to make recommendations on U.S. policy toward Afghanistan. The full text of their report is available on the foundation's Web site.

Afghanistan Relief Organization (ARO)
PO Box 10207, Canoga Park, CA 91304
(818) 709-7011
Web site: www.afghanrelief.org

ARO was established in 1997 in response to the economic and physical hardships suffered by the Afghan people after decades of war. It is a volunteer organization funded by public donations that takes blankets, clothing, tents, and hygiene and other relief supplies to the poorest people in Afghanistan. The organization collects donations from American schools under its School Supply Project, which is designed to help educate Afghan youth who have lived their whole lives in wars and violent conflicts. The organization provides information on how to contact Afghan Americans for interviews or help with research on Afghanistan.

Afghanistan Research and Evaluation Unit (AREU)
Charahi Ansari, Kabul, Afghanistan
(882) 168-980-0144
e-mail: areu@areu.org.pk • Web site: www.areu.org.pk

AREU is an independent organization that conducts action-oriented research to assist in formulation of government policies for reconstruction and development in Afghanistan. AREU was established by the international aid community in 2002, and has representatives from the United Nations and government and nongovernment organizations on its advisory board. Its Web site features a number of publications including *Urban Livelihoods of Nine Kabul Households* and *How Government Works in Afghanistan.*

American Enterprise Institute for Public Policy Research (AEI)
1150 Seventeenth St. NW, Washington, DC 20036
(202) 862-5800
Web site: www.aei.org

AEI is a conservative research and education organization that studies national and international issues, including American foreign policy. It promotes the spread of democracy and believes the United States should continue to be a world leader. Among its many activities, AEI hosts conferences in Washington, D.C., to bring together scholars and government officials to discuss U.S. policy in Afghanistan. Papers from these conferences are available on its Web site as well as the latest news and commentary on Afghanistan. AEI publishes the monthlies *American Enterprise* and *AEI Economist*, the bimonthly *Public Opinion*, and various books on America's foreign policy.

America's Fund for Afghan Children (AFAC)
c/o The White House, 1600 Pennsylvania Ave. NW, Washington, DC 20509-1600
Web site: www.kidsfund.redcross.org

In October 2001 President George W. Bush announced the creation of America's Fund for Afghan Children in response to the concern expressed by Americans for the plight of the children in war-torn Afghanistan. In order to help provide food, shelter, education, and health care for Afghan children, the president asked that each American child contribute one dollar to the fund. AFAC funds are administered by the American Red Cross, which reports on the fund's activities on its Web site.

CARE
151 Ellis St. NE, Atlanta, GA 30303-2439
(800) 521-2273, ext. 999
Web site: www.care.org

As one of the world's largest international relief and development organizations, CARE reaches more than 35 million people in more than sixty developing nations in Africa, Asia, Latin America, and Europe. CARE works to provide basic education and immunization for children, economic and social empowerment for women, a stable supply of food and clean water, basic health care, and access to family planning services. CARE publishes an annual report and special reports on individual countries. Special reports on current events and CARE programs in Afghanistan are available on its Web site.

Cato Institute
1000 Massachussetts Ave. NW, Washington, DC 20001-5403
(202) 842-0200
e-mail: cato@cato.org • Web site: www.cato.org

The institute is a libertarian public policy research foundation dedicated to stimulating foreign policy debate. It publishes the triannual *Cato Journal*, the periodic *Cato Policy Analysis*, and a bimonthly newsletter *Cato Policy Review*. Cato's Web site on terrorism includes articles on Afghanistan, the war on drugs, and recommendations for U.S. policies in central and south Asia.

Center for Afghanistan Studies (CAS)
University of Nebraska, 6001 Dodge St., Omaha, NE 68182
(402) 554-2800
Web site: www.unomaha.edu

Established in 1972 at the University of Nebraska, the CAS provides scholarly exchanges, technical assistance, and training to educational institutions in Afghanistan. With its field office in Kabul, CAS acts as a focal point for gathering together significant source materials and for contacts between Afghan specialists from around the world. The center publishes the *Afghanistan Studies Journal.*

EurasiaNet.Org
e-mail: info@eurasianet.org • Web site: www.eurasianet.org

EurasiaNet.org provides information and analysis of political, economic, environmental, and social developments in countries in central Asia, the Caucasus, the Middle East, southwest Asia, and in Russia. The organization publishes an online journal, *Eurasia Insight*, which includes articles designed to inform policy makers in the United States and in the targeted regions on current events.

Help the Afghan Children International (HTACI)
8603 Westwood Center Dr., Suite 230, Vienna, VA 22182
(888) 403-0407
Web site: www.helptheafghanchildren.org

In 1993 Afghan American Suraya Sadeed established HTACI, a nonprofit organization designed to help Afghan women and children. The organization funds primary health-care clinics, educational and vocational training projects, and innovative programs like peace education and environmental awareness. HTACI's publications include the *Voice of Innocence Newsletter*, which describes the organization's activities and includes articles on the latest developments in Afghanistan.

Human Rights Watch (HRW)
350 Fifth Ave., 34th Floor, New York, NY 10118-3299
(212) 290-4700
e-mail: hrwnyc@hrw.org • Web site: www.hrw.org

HRW is the largest human rights organization in the United States. With offices in New York, Washington, D.C., Los Angeles, San Francisco, Brussels, London, and Geneva, HRW staff research and conduct fact-finding missions into human rights abuses in more than seventy countries. In July 2003 the organization published a controversial article, "Killing You Is a Very Easy Thing for Us to Do," about the continued human rights abuses in Afghanistan after the fall of the Taliban. Its publication *World Development Report 2004: Human Rights and Armed Conflicts* includes essays on Afghanistan.

Institute for Afghan Studies (IAS)
Web site: www.institute-for-afghan-studies.org

Founded and run by young Afghan scholars from around the world, the goal of IAS is to promote a better understanding of Afghan affairs through scholarly research and studies. The IAS Web site gives information on the history and politics of Afghanistan, and provides biographical information on key Afghan and Taliban leaders.

Islamic Transitional State of Afghanistan
Web site: www.afghanistangov.org

This central Web site of the Afghanistan government provides information on Afghanistan's budget, on international aid, and on major international conferences. It gives profiles of the government plans in the major sectors and contains links to all the main government agencies. Government reports, ministers' speeches, and biodata on key Afghan figures can be accessed through its Web site.

Muslim Public Affairs Council (MPAC)
3010 Wilshire Blvd., Suite 217, Los Angeles, CA 90010
(213) 383-3443
e-mail: salam@mpac.org • Web site: www.mpac.org

MPAC is a nonprofit, public service agency that strives to disseminate in the United States accurate information about Muslims and achieve cooperation between various communities on the basis of shared values such as peace, justice, freedom, and dignity. It publishes and distributes a number of reports on issues of concern to the Muslim community, such as reports on U.S. foreign relations and human rights policy. MPAC publishes *Minaret*, an online journal on Islamic affairs, and position papers on current issues.

Revolutionary Association of the Women of Afghanistan (RAWA)
PO Box 374, Quetta, Pakistan
(0092) (300) 855-1638
e-mail: rawa@rawa.org • Web site: www.rawa.org

Established in 1977 in Kabul, RAWA is an organization of Afghan women who are dedicated to peace, freedom, democracy, human rights, and social justice. The organization solicits public donations for relief aid and for projects to assist schools, orphanages, and women's cooperatives. RAWA's Web site includes press reports and journal articles on political, economic, and social issues in Afghanistan. Its recent publications include Anne Brodsky's *With All Our Strength: The Revolutionary Association of the Women of Afghanistan*, and Melody Ermachild Chavis's *Meena: Heroine of Afghanistan: The Martyr Who Founded RAWA.*

United Nations Assistance Mission to Afghanistan (UNAMA)
PO Box 5858, Grand Central Station, New York, NY 10163-5858
e-mail: spokesman-unama@un.org • Web site: www.unama-afg.org

In 2002 the United Nations Security Council established UNAMA to integrate the activities of the sixteen UN agencies in Afghanistan. UNAMA's mandate includes promoting national reconciliation and human rights, and managing humanitarian relief projects. UNAMA has its head office in Kabul and has regional offices in the major provinces. Key UN documents and speeches by UN personnel on Afghanistan can be found on its Web site.

United Nations Development Programme (UNDP)
1 United Nations Plaza, New York, NY 10017
(212) 906-5315 • fax: (212) 906-5001
e-mail: HQ@undp.org • Web site: www.undp.org

The UNDP is committed to the principle that development is inseparable from the quest for peace and human security and that the United Nations must be a strong force for development as well as for peace. UNDP aims to help member nations achieve sustainable human development through providing technical assistance and training for people in developing countries. The organization publishes *Beyond Aid: Questions and Answers for a Post–Cold War World*, and the quarterly magazine *Choices*. Information on UNDP projects in Afghanistan is available on its Web site.

United States–Afghan Women's Council
fax: (202) 312-9663
e-mail: Hovanecsc@state.gov • Web site: http://usawc.state.gov

In February 2002 President George W. Bush and Afghan president Hamid Karzai announced the creation of the United States–Afghan Women's Council to promote cooperative ventures between women in their two countries to help Afghan women gain an education and find employment. The council is cochaired by the U.S. undersecretary for global affairs and the Afghan ministers of women's affairs and foreign affairs, and is staffed by the U.S. Department of State Office of International Women's Issues. Its Web site includes information on council projects, and speeches and press releases on Afghan women's issues.

United States Agency for International Development (USAID)
Ronald Reagan Building, Washington, DC 20523-0016
(202) 712-4810
Web site: www.usaid.gov

USAID is the U.S. government agency that implements America's foreign economic and humanitarian assistance programs and provides asistance to countries recovering from disaster, trying to escape poverty, and engaging in democratic reforms. USAID is an independent federal government agency that receives overall foreign policy guidance from the secretary of state. The agency provides information on its policies and programs in Afghanistan on its Web site.

United States Department of State
Office of Public Communications
Public Information Service Bureau of Public Affairs, Washington, DC 20520
(202) 647-6575
e-mail: secretary@state.gov • Web site: www.state.gov

The Department of State advises the president in the formulation and execution of foreign policy, and includes the Bureau for International Narcotics and Law Enforcement Affairs, and the U.S. Counterterrorism Office, both of which manage programs in Afghanistan. Information on these programs and speeches by government officials are available on the department's Web site.

World Bank
1818 H St. NW, Washington, DC 20433
(202) 477-1234
Web site: www.worldbank.org

The World Bank is the world's largest source of development assistance funds, providing more than $18 billion in loans to its client countries in 2003–2004. The bank uses its financial resources and extensive knowledge base to help developing countries move to a path of stable, sustainable, and equitable growth. The organization publishes many books and reports, including *The World Development Report*, which gives a global perspective on the developing world, and individual country studies, including studies on Afghanistan's economic performance and prospects. A special section on the bank Web site features policy papers on Afghanistan, and provides information on World Bank projects in Afghanistan in the agriculture, health, education, and economic sectors.

Bibliography

Books

Ludwig W. Adamec	*Historical Dictionary of Afghanistan.* Lanham, MD: Scarecrow Press, 2003.
Akbar S. Ahmed	*Discovering Islam: Making Sense of Muslim History and Society.* New York: Routledge, 2002.
Akbar S. Ahmed	*Islam Under Siege: Living Dangerously in a Post-Honor World.* New Delhi, India: Vistaar, 2003.
Sultan Barakat, ed.	*Reconstructing War-Torn Societies: Afghanistan.* New York: Palgrove Macmillan, 2004.
Cheryl Benard	*Veiled Courage: Inside the Afghan Women's Resistance.* New York: Broadway Books, 2002.
Anne E. Brodsky	*With All Our Strength: The Revolutionary Association of the Women of Afghanistan.* New York: Routledge, 2003.
James Dobbins, ed.	*America's Role in Nation-Building.* Santa Monica, CA: Rand, 2003.
Antonio Donini, Norah Niland, and Karin Wermester, eds.	*Nation-Building Unraveled: Aid, Peace, and Justice in Afghanistan.* Bloomfield, CT: Kumarin Press, 2004.
Louis Dupree	*Afghanistan.* Princeton, NJ: Princeton University Press, 1980.
Thomas Dworzak	*Taliban.* London: Trolley, 2003.
Martin Ewans	*Afghanistan: A Short History of Its People and Politics.* New York: HarperCollins, 2002.
M.J. Gohari	*The Taliban: Ascent to Power.* London: Oxford University Press, 2000.
Edward Grazda	*Afghanistan Diary 1992–2000.* New York: PowerHouse Books, 2000.
Victor Davis Hanson	*Between War and Peace: Lessons from Afghanistan to Iraq.* New York: Random House, 2004.
Asma Gull Hasan	*Why I Am a Muslim: An Amercian Odyssey.* San Francisco: Thorsons Element, 2004.

Bibliography

Christina Lamb   *The Sewing Circles of Herat: My Afghan Years.* London: HarperCollins, 2002.

David W. Lesch, ed.   *The Middle East and the United States: A Historical and Political Reassessment.* Boulder, CO: Westview Press, 2003.

Bernard Lewis   *What Went Wrong?: Western Impact and Middle Eastern Response.* New York: Oxford University Press, 2002.

Ernest Karl Meyer   *The Dust of Empire: The Race for Mastery in the Asian Heartland.* New York: Public Affairs, 2003.

Amelendu Misra   *Afghanistan: A Labyrinth of Violence.* Malden, MA: Polity, 2004.

John Norton Moore   *Solving the War Puzzle: Beyond the Democratic Peace.* Durham, NC: Carolina Academic Press, 2004.

Angelo Rasanayagam   *Afghanistan: A Modern History: Monarchy, Despotism, or Democracy? The Problems of Governance in the Muslim Tradition.* New York: I.B. Tauris, 2003.

Ahmed Rashid   *Islam, Oil, and the New Great Game in Central Asia.* London: I.B. Tauris, 2000.

Ahmed Rashid   *Jihad: The Rise of Militant Islam in Central Asia.* New Haven, CT: Yale University Press, 2002.

Paul Rogers   *A War on Terror: Afghanistan and After.* Sterling, VA: Pluto Press, 2004.

Barnett Rubin   *The Fragmentation of Afghanistan: State Formation and Collapse in the International System.* New Haven, CT: Yale University Press, 2002.

Peter Dale Scott   *Drugs, Oil, and War: The United States in Afghanistan, Colombia, and Indochina.* Lanham, MD: Rowman and Littlefield, 2003.

Batya Swift Yasgur   *Behind the Burqa: Our Life in Afghanistan and How We Escaped to Freedom.* Hoboken, NJ: John Wiley, 2002.

Periodicals

Mark Berniker   "Afghanistan Stands on the Brink of Becoming a 'Narco-State,'" *Eurasia Insight*, February 10, 2004.

Scott Carrier   "Childhood Burdens," *Mother Jones*, July/August 2002.

David Corn   "Bush's Afghan Disgrace," *AlterNet*, November 15, 2002. www.alternet.org.

Joseph Curl   "Afghan Leader Seeks U.S. Aid with Stability," *Washington Post*, April 14, 2003.

Simon Denyer   "Reality in Afghanistan Belies U.S. Rhetoric," *Dawn*, May 9, 2003.

Lynette Dumble   "Afghanistan: Report Exposes Continuing Human Rights Abuses," *Green Left Weekly*, August 13, 2003.

181

Afghanistan

Eve Ensler — "This Is a Most Fragile Time for Afghanistan," *Women's ENEWS*, May 2, 2003. www.womensenews.org.

Golnaz Esfandiari — "Self-Immolation of Women on the Rise in Western Provinces," *RFE/RL*, March 1, 2004. www.rferl.org.

Robert Evans — "Climate of Fear Rules Afghanistan," Reuters, April 22, 2003.

Martin Ewans — "How Stands Afghanistan Now?" *World & I*, July 2003.

Conor Foley and Mark Lattimer — "The New Tragedy in Afghanistan," *Guardian*, December 10, 2003.

Carlotta Gall — "In Afghanistan, Violence Stalls Renewal Effort," *New York Times*, April 26, 2003.

Linda S. Heard — "Apathy of Afghan Women After Taliban," *Gulf News*, September 23, 2003.

Stephanie Hiller — "Author Finds Little Progress in Afghanistan," *Awakened Woman*, July 25, 2003.

Isabel Hilton — "Now We Pay the Warlords to Tyrannise the Afghan People," *Guardian*, July 31, 2003.

Judith Huber — "Afghanistan: The Taliban's Smiling Face," *La Monde Diplomatique*, March 2003.

Mark Kaufman — "U.S. Lands in Middle of Afghan Feuding," *Washington Post*, March 28, 2003.

Jonathon Ledgard — "Border Clashes Open New Afghan Front Line," *Telegraph Group Limited*, July 18, 2003.

Jim Lobe — "Hamid, Hamid Who?" *Asia Times*, March 7, 2003.

Sean M. Maloney — "Afghanistan: From Here to Eternity," *Parameters*, Spring 2004.

Rob Moll — "Taliban II? Religious Rights Watchers Are Deeply Troubled by the Afghan Constitution," *Christianity Today*, March 2004.

Ron Moreau and Faisal Enayat Khan — "Walking a Fine Line," *Newsweek International*, June 9, 2003.

Samantha Nutt — "Freedom Denied: When the Taliban Fell Women Were Supposed to Get a Better Deal. It Hasn't Happened," *Maclean's*, July 1, 2003.

Gordon Peake — "From Warlords to Peacelords?" *Journal of International Affairs*, Spring 2003.

John Pilger — "Bush's Vietnam: The Rapacious Adventures in Iraq and Afghanistan Are Going Badly Wrong," *New Statesman*, June 23, 2003.

Ahmed Rashid — "Afghanistan Torn as Its Neighbours Resume Their Battle for Influence," *Telegraph* (London), February 10, 2003.

Ahmed Rashid — "The Betrayal of the Afghans," *New York Review of Books*, January 29, 2004.

Bibliography

Paul M. Rodriguez — "Afghans Embrace a Source of Hope," *Insight on the News*, February 2, 2004.

Jake Rupert — "Afghan Editor Forced to Flee to Canada," *National Post* (Canada), October 27, 2003.

Salman Rushdie — "Anti-Americanism Has Taken the World by Storm," *Guardian*, February 6, 2002.

Syed Saleem Shahzad — "Afghanistan Once More the Melting Pot," *Asia Times*, May 1, 2003.

Frederick Starr — "A Sweet Sixteen: Plenty of Reasons to Cheer Post-Taliban Afghanistan," *National Review*, August 11, 2003.

Washington Times — "Afghan Aid: More Is Better Only If Well-Spent," August 26, 2003.

April Witt — "Afghans Rally in Anger Towards U.S.," *Washington Post*, May 7, 2003.

Phil Zabriskie and Spin Boldak — "Undefeated," *TimeAsia*, July 21, 2003.

Index

Index

Stephens, Philip, 90
Straw, Jack, 32

Tajiks, 31
Taliban
Afghanistan under, 108–109
resurgence of, 14
human rights abuses and, 69–70
is exaggerated, 33–34
threatens reconstruction effort, 35–38, 113
source of support for, 31
targets of, 36–37
U.S. attacks on, 17
women's status under, 53, 62–63
Tamerlane, 94
Taniwal, Hakim, 114
Taraki, Nur Mohammed, 106
Tarzi, Amin, 42
terrorism
issues behind, 109
U.S. must aid Afghanistan to combat, 105–109
U.S. should focus on, 118–19
Thatcher, Margaret, 88
Thomas, Luke, 166
Time (magazine), 37

United Nations
in postinvasion Afghanistan, 18
role in building political institutions, 28
Security Council goals for Afghanistan, 111–12
survey of poppy cultivation, 48–49
United Nations Assistance Mission in Afghanistan (UNAMA), 72
United Nations Children's Fund (UNICEF), 58, 59, 60
exaggerates its achievements, 76
United Nations High Commissioner on Refugees (UNHCR), 65, 67, 83–84
United States
Afghan aid efforts of, 97
spending on, 19, 28, 133
hurts poor in U.S., 133–34
vs. Afghanistan, in establishment of democracy, 150
has failed to provide security, 72

has poor record with democracy, 163–64, 172–74
invasion by, 17–18
Afghan poor are victims of, 78
post-WWII relations with Afghanistan, 105–106
record of nation-building by, 116–17
should leave Afghanistan, 120–29
should pursue nation building in Afghanistan, 105–109
con, 110–19
support of warlords by, 80–81
see also U.S. forces
UNOCAL, 108
U.S. forces
resentment against, 114–15
role of, 21–22
U.S. hides casualties among, 124–25

warlords, 30
democracy is undermined by, 39–41, 110
elections can strengthen, 172, 173
human rights abuses by, 69–70
retain control of Afghanistan, 74, 75–76
rivalries among, threaten recovery, 113–14
U.S. alliance with, 21, 32, 80–81
Washington Post (newspaper), 21, 97, 112
Witt, April, 46
Wolsei Jirga, 166
women
in *Loya Jirga*, 27
vs. men, educational achievement of, 157
role of, in Islam, 164–65
successes in improving lives of, 58–60, 61–64
have been limited, 70, 77, 79–81
under Taliban regime, 53, 62–63
voting by, 26
Woodward, Susan, 171
World Bank, 19, 89
World Food Program (WFP), 67

Yasini, Yarwais, 50

Zabriskie, Phil, 35
Zadran, Bacha Khan, 114
Zakhilwal, Omar, 39